Company's Coming®

COOKIES

by
Jean Paré

Dedication

*For everyone who has ever been caught
with a hand in the cookie jar.*

Cover Photo

COOKIES

Eleventh Printing, December, 1993

I.S.B.N. 0-9690695-8-8

Published and Distributed by
Company's Coming Publishing Limited
Box 8037, Station "F"
Edmonton, Alberta, Canada
T6H 4N9

**Published Simultaneously in
Canada and the United States of America**

Printed In Canada

Company's Coming Cookbooks
by Jean Paré

table of Contents

Jean Paré was born and raised during the Great Depression in Irma, a small rural town in eastern Alberta, Canada. She grew up understanding that the combination of family, friends and home cooking is the essence of a good life. Jean learned from her mother, Ruby Elford, to appreciate good cooking and was encouraged by her father, Edward Elford, who praised even her earliest attempts. When she left home she took with her many acquired family recipes, her love of cooking and her intriguing desire to read recipe books like novels!

While raising a family of four, Jean was always busy in her kitchen preparing delicious, tasty treats and savory meals for family and friends of all ages. Her reputation flourished as the mom who would happily feed the neighborhood.

In 1963, when her children had all reached school age, Jean volunteered to cater to the 50th anniversary of the Vermilion School of Agriculture, now Lakeland College. Working out of her home, Jean prepared a dinner for over 1000 people which launched a flourishing catering operation that continued for over eighteen years. During that time she was provided with countless opportunities to test new ideas with immediate feedback – resulting in empty plates and contented customers! Whether preparing cocktail sandwiches for a house party or serving a hot meal for 1500 people, Jean Paré earned a reputation for good food, courteous service and reasonable prices.

"Why don't you write a cookbook?" Time and again, as requests for her recipes mounted, Jean was asked that question. Jean's response was to team up with her son Grant Lovig in the fall of 1980 to form Company's Coming Publishing Limited. April 14, 1981, marked the debut of "150 DELICIOUS SQUARES", the first Company's Coming cookbook in what soon would become Canada's most popular cookbook series. Jean released a new title each year for the first six years. The pace quickened and by 1987 the company had begun publishing two titles each year.

Jean Paré's operation has grown from the early days of working out of a spare bedroom in her home to operating a large and fully equipped test kitchen in Vermilion, Alberta, near the home she and her husband Larry built. Full time staff has grown steadily to include marketing personnel located in major cities across Canada plus selected U.S. markets. Home Office is located in Edmonton, Alberta where distribution, accounting and administration functions are headquartered in the company's own recently constructed 20,000 square foot facility. Company's Coming cookbooks are now distributed throughout Canada and the United States plus numerous overseas markets. Translation of the series to the Spanish and French languages began in 1990. Pint Size Books followed in 1993, offering a smaller, less expensive format focusing on more specialized topics. The recipes continued in the familiar and trusted Company's Coming style.

Jean Paré's approach to cooking has always called for easy-to-follow recipes using mostly common, affordable ingredients. Her wonderful collection of time-honored recipes, many of which are family heirlooms, is a welcome addition to any kitchen. That's why we say: "taste the tradition".

$\mathcal{F}$oreword

Visions of all kinds are conjured up at the very mention of the word "cookies". Opening the door upon arriving home from school to the heavenly aroma of freshly baked cookies leaves an indelible print in one's mind. Baking a batch of cookies will bring back enthusiasm to youngsters who are "dying of boredom".

Of course there are memories of sneaking a few forbidden cookies as well as taking "just one" from the freezer day after day until somehow the freezer carton is nearly empty. Some deeds can't be covered up.

This book contains many varieties. Ice box cookies that are made one day and baked the next are always enjoyed. Drop cookies such as Hermits and Chocolate Nuggets are great for lunch and snacks. Fancy tea rolls such as Brandy Snaps make a fussy "tea" complete.

Every cookie in this book is pictured in full color. Browse through at your leisure and choose an assortment of shapes and sizes for baking. Planning ahead? Every cookie can be frozen.

Baking time varies due to the thickness and size of each cookie. Overbaking causes dryness and hardness. Room must be left for expansion. If baking sheets have sides, turn upside down and use bottoms. This makes cookies easier to remove from the pan. When using two baking sheets in your oven at the same time, exchange the top sheet with the bottom sheet and reverse both from front to back half way through baking.

When company's coming — any age or any size of crowd — be ready for the onslaught with a full cookie jar.

Jean Paré

FLORENTINES

An elegant cookie! Bottoms are spread with chocolate. Contain almonds and peel.

Butter or margarine	¼ cup	60 mL
Granulated sugar	½ cup	125 mL
Whipping cream	¼ cup	60 mL
All–purpose flour	2 tbsp.	30 mL
Flaked almonds	1 cup	225 mL
Candied orange peel, finely chopped	½ cup	125 mL
Chopped candied cherries	2 tbsp.	30 mL
Semisweet chocolate chips	½ cup	125 mL

In small saucepan combine butter, sugar and cream. Heat, stirring until it boils. Remove from heat.

Stir in flour, almonds, orange peel and cherries. Drop 2 measuring tsp. (10 mL) per cookie onto greased baking sheet. Spread with spoon. Bake in 350°F (180°C) oven for 10 to 12 minutes. With pancake lifter, push in edges a bit all around to make a good neat edge. Let stand until you are able to remove them without tearing, about 3 or 4 minutes. Cool.

Melt chips in heavy saucepan over low heat. Spread flat side (bottom) of cookies with chocolate. Let stand ½ hour. Crease in wavy lines with fork. Makes 2 dozen.

Pictured on page 143.

Naturally you would expect homeless dogs to be in an arf–anage.

PUMPKIN COOKIES

A spicy drop that is economical as well as popular.

Butter or margarine, softened	1/2 cup	125 mL
Brown sugar, packed	1 1/4 cups	300 mL
Eggs	2	2
Vanilla	1 tsp.	5 mL
Canned pumpkin (or fresh cooked and mashed)	1 cup	250 mL
All–purpose flour	2 cups	500 mL
Baking powder	4 tsp.	20 ml
Salt	1/2 tsp.	2 mL
Cinnamon	1/2 tsp.	2 mL
Nutmeg	1/2 tsp.	2 mL
Cloves	1/4 tsp.	1 mL
Ginger	1/4 tsp.	1 mL
Raisins or chocolate chips	1 cup	250 mL
Chopped nuts	1 cup	250 mL

Cream butter and sugar together well. Beat in eggs 1 at a time. Add vanilla and pumpkin.

Stir remaining ingredients together and add. Mix well. Drop by table–spoonfuls onto greased pan. Bake in 375°F (190°C) oven for about 15 minutes until lightly browned. Makes 5 1/2 dozen.

Pictured on page 71.

ORANGE COCONUT COOKIES

The flavor of coconut comes through well in these.

Butter or margarine, softened	1 cup	250 mL
Grated orange rind	2 tbsp.	30 mL
Granulated sugar	1 1/4 cups	300 mL
Eggs	2	2
Milk	1/4 cup	60 mL
All–purpose flour	2 cups	500 mL
Baking powder	2 1/4 tsp.	11 mL
Cinnamon	3/4 tsp.	4 mL
Salt	1/4 tsp.	1 mL
Rolled oats	1 cup	250 mL
Shredded coconut	3/4 cup	175 mL

(continued on next page)

Cream butter, orange rind and sugar together well. Beat in eggs 1 at a time. Add milk.

Stir flour, baking powder, cinnamon and salt together and add. Mix together.

Stir in oats and coconut. Drop by spoonfuls onto greased baking sheet. Bake in 400°F (200°C) oven for 8 to 10 minutes. Makes 4 dozen.

Pictured on page 71.

CORNFLAKE COOKIES

Resembles a butter cookie with spice added.

Butter or margarine, softened	½ cup	125 mL
Granulated sugar	½ cup	125 mL
Brown sugar, packed	½ cup	125 mL
Egg	1	1
Vanilla	½ tsp.	2 mL
All–purpose flour	1 cup	250 mL
Baking powder	1 tsp.	5 mL
Salt	¼ tsp.	1 mL
Cinnamon	½ tsp.	2 mL
Ginger	¼ tsp.	1 mL
Nutmeg	¼ tsp.	1 mL
Cloves	⅛ tsp.	0.5 mL
Cornflakes	1½ cups	375 mL
Chopped dates or raisins (optional)	1 cup	250 mL

Cream butter and both sugars together. Beat in egg and vanilla.

Add remaining ingredients. Mix well. Drop by spoonfuls onto greased baking sheet. Bake in 350°F (180°C) oven for 10 to 12 minutes. Makes 2½ to 3 dozen.

Pictured on page 71.

ORANGE BRAN COOKIES

A wonderful breakfast cookie.

Butter or margarine, softened	½ cup	125 mL
Granulated sugar	½ cup	125 mL
Egg	1	1
Prepared orange juice	2 tbsp.	30 mL
Grated orange rind	1½ tsp.	7 mL
All–purpose flour	1 cup	250 mL
Baking powder	1 tsp.	5 mL
Salt	½ tsp.	2 mL
Bran flakes cereal	1 cup	250 mL
Semisweet chocolate chips (optional)	1 cup	250 mL

Cream butter and sugar together. Beat in egg. Add orange juice and rind.

Add remaining ingredients. Mix well. Drop by spoonfuls onto greased cookie sheet. Bake in 350°F (180°C) oven for 10 to 12 minutes. Makes 3 dozen.

Pictured on cover.

PEANUT MOLASSES COOKIES

A different flavor combination.

Butter or margarine, softened	½ cup	125 mL
Granulated sugar	½ cup	125 mL
Egg	1	1
Smooth peanut butter	¾ cup	175 mL
Table molasses	½ cup	125 mL
All–purpose flour	1¼ cups	300 mL
Rolled oats	1 cup	250 mL
Baking powder	2 tsp.	10 mL
Baking soda	¼ tsp.	1 mL
Salt	½ tsp.	2 mL

Cream butter and sugar together well. Beat in egg. Mix in peanut butter and molasses.

Stir remaining ingredients together and add. Mix well. Drop by spoon–fuls onto ungreased baking sheet. Flatten with floured glass or with fork. Bake in 375°F (190°C) oven for 12 to 15 minutes. Makes about 3 dozen.

Pictured on page 71.

BUTTERSCOTCH OAT DROPS

The addition of butterscotch chips makes these doubly good.

Butter or margarine, softened	1 cup	250 mL
Granulated sugar	½ cup	125 mL
Brown sugar, packed	1 cup	250 mL
Eggs	2	2
Vanilla	1 tsp.	5 mL
All–purpose flour	2 cups	500 mL
Rolled oats	2 cups	500 mL
Baking soda	1 tsp.	5 mL
Baking powder	1 tsp.	5 mL
Salt	1 tsp.	5 mL
Butterscotch chips	2 cups	500 mL
Chopped nuts (optional)	1 cup	250 mL

Combine butter and both sugars in bowl. Cream well. Beat in eggs 1 at a time. Add vanilla.

Measure in remaining ingredients. Mix together. Drop by spoonfuls onto ungreased baking sheet. Bake in 350°F (180°C) oven for 8 to 10 minutes. Makes 6 dozen.

Pictured on page 53.

Paré Pointer

Cross a Pekingese and a Pomeranian and you will have a peeking pom.

ANZAC COOKIES

These are crisp with a rich caramel color and taste. Popular "down under".

All–purpose flour	1 cup	225 mL
Granulated sugar	1 cup	225 mL
Rolled oats	1 cup	225 mL
Coconut	1 cup	225 mL
Butter or margarine, melted	1/2 cup	125 mL
Golden syrup	2 tbsp.	30 mL
Baking soda	1 tsp.	5 mL
Boiling water	1/4 cup	60 mL

Put flour, sugar, oats and coconut into mixing bowl. Stir together. Make a well in center.

Add butter and syrup to well.

Dissolve baking soda in water. Add to well. Mix. Drop by spoonfuls onto greased baking sheet. Bake in 350°F (180°C) oven for about 8 to 10 minutes. Makes 3 dozen.

Pictured on page 53.

BANANA OATMEAL COOKIES

Banana with dates are a natural.

Butter or margarine, softened	3/4 cup	175 mL
Granulated sugar	1 cup	250 mL
Egg	1	1
Mashed banana	1 cup	250 mL
All–purpose flour	1 1/2 cups	375 mL
Salt	1 tsp.	5 mL
Baking soda	1/2 tsp.	2 mL
Cinnamon	1 tsp.	5 mL
Nutmeg	1/4 tsp.	1 mL
Rolled oats	1 3/4 cups	425 mL
Chopped nuts	1/2 cup	125 mL
Chopped dates	1 cup	250 mL

(continued on next page)

Cream butter and sugar together well. Beat in egg. Add banana.

Stir remaining ingredients together and add. Mix well. Drop by spoon–fuls onto greased baking sheet. Bake in 400°F (200°C) oven for 10 to 12 minutes. Makes 4½ dozen.

Pictured on page 89.

RAISIN NUT DROPS

These can be dropped or rolled into balls. They are moist, chewy, good.

Butter or margarine, softened	1 cup	250 mL
Granulated sugar	1 cup	250 mL
Brown sugar, packed	1 cup	250 mL
Eggs	2	2
Vanilla	1 tsp.	5 mL
Rum flavoring	1 tsp.	5 mL
Raisins, ground	1 cup	250 mL
Walnuts, ground	1 cup	250 mL
Rolled oats, ground	1 cup	250 ml
All–purpose flour	2¼ cups	560 mL
Baking soda	1½ tsp.	7 mL
Salt	¼ tsp.	1 mL

In large bowl, cream butter and both sugars together. Beat in eggs 1 at a time. Add vanilla and rum flavoring.

Put raisins, walnuts and rolled oats through grinder or use food processor. Add to batter and mix in.

Stir flour, baking soda and salt together and mix in. Either drop from spoon or roll into small balls and place on greased baking sheet. Bake in 350°F (180°C) oven for 7 to 8 minutes. Makes 6 dozen.

Pictured on page 71.

KRUNCHY KRISPS

Crispy and crunchy. A good cookie jar filler.

Butter or margarine, softened	**1 cup**	**250 mL**
Granulated sugar	**¾ cup**	**175 mL**
Brown sugar, packed	**¾ cup**	**175 mL**
Eggs	**2**	**2**
Vanilla	**1 tsp.**	**5 mL**
All-purpose flour	**1½ cups**	**375 mL**
Rolled oats	**1½ cups**	**375 mL**
Coconut	**½ cup**	**125 mL**
Cinnamon	**1 tsp.**	**5 mL**
Baking powder	**1 tsp.**	**5 mL**
Baking soda	**½ tsp.**	**2 mL**

Cream butter and both sugars together in mixing bowl. Beat in eggs and vanilla.

Stir in remaining ingredients. Drop by spoonfuls onto lightly greased cookie sheet. Bake in 375°F (190°C) oven for about 10 minutes until browned. Makes about 5 dozen.

Pictured on page 125.

SPICY OATMEAL COOKIES

These cookies are chewy and rich in color.

Butter or margarine, softened	½ cup	125 mL
Granulated sugar	1 cup	250 mL
Eggs	2	2
Molasses	⅓ cup	75 mL
All–purpose flour	1¾ cups	425 mL
Baking soda	1 tsp.	5 mL
Salt	½ tsp.	2 mL
Cinnamon	1½ tsp.	7 mL
Raisins	1 cup	250 mL
Chopped nuts	½ cup	125 mL
Rolled oats	2 cups	500 mL

Cream butter and sugar together. Beat in eggs 1 at a time. Add molasses.

Add remaining ingredients. Mix well. Drop by spoonfuls onto greased baking sheet. Bake in 350°F (180°C) oven for 8 to 10 minutes. Makes about 5 dozen.

Pictured on page 89.

ORANGE COOKIES

These contain raisins for added goodness.

Butter or margarine, softened	½ cup	125 mL
Granulated sugar	1 cup	250 mL
Eggs	2	2
Orange flavoring	2 tsp.	10 mL
Milk	¼ cup	60 mL
All–purpose flour	2 cups	450 mL
Baking powder	2 tsp.	10 mL
Grated orange rind	1 tbsp.	15 mL
Raisins	1 cup	250 mL

Cream butter and sugar together. Beat in eggs 1 at a time. Add orange flavoring and milk.

Add flour, baking powder, orange rind and raisins. Mix well. Drop by spoonfuls onto greased cookie sheet. Bake in 375°F (190°C) oven for 8 to 10 minutes. Makes 3½ dozen.

Pictured on page 53.

HERMITS

One of the best known drop cookies. Cookie jars are filled with these for after school snacks.

Butter or margarine, softened	1 cup	250 mL
Brown sugar, packed	1½ cups	375 mL
Eggs	3	3
Vanilla	1 tsp.	5 mL
All–purpose flour	3 cups	750 mL
Baking powder	1 tsp.	5 mL
Baking soda	1 tsp.	5 mL
Salt	½ tsp.	2 mL
Cinnamon	1 tsp.	5 mL
Nutmeg	½ tsp.	2 mL
Allspice	¼ tsp.	1 mL
Raisins	1 cup	250 mL
Chopped dates	1 cup	250 mL
Chopped nuts	⅔ cup	150 mL

Cream butter and sugar together. Beat in eggs 1 at a time. Add vanilla.

Measure in remaining ingredients. Mix well. Drop onto greased bak–ing sheet by heaping teaspoonfuls. Bake in 375°F (190°C) oven for 6 to 8 minutes. Makes 4½ dozen.

Pictured on page 125.

MACAROONS

Chewy little stacks. Use the longest coconut you can find.

Egg whites	3	3
Granulated sugar	¾ cup	175 mL
Cornstarch	2 tbsp.	30 mL
Salt	⅛ tsp.	0.5 mL
Coconut, long threaded (approximately ⅔ lb., 300 g)	4 cups	900 mL

In top of double boiler on counter, beat egg whites until stiff and dry. Place over boiling water.

(continued on next page)

Stir sugar, cornstarch and salt together. Add to whites. Stir to mix. Cook until crust forms around edge, about 5 minutes. Remove from heat.

Add coconut to thicken. Shape into balls. Drop by spoonfuls onto greased baking sheet. Bake in 350°F (180°C) oven for about 12 to 15 minutes until slightly browned. Makes about 3½ dozen cookies.

Pictured on page 53.

HONEY OATMEAL COOKIES

Soft and golden, studded with raisins.

Butter or margarine, softened	¾ cup	175 mL
Granulated sugar	½ cup	125 mL
Soft honey	½ cup	125 mL
Egg	1	1
Vanilla	1 tsp.	5 mL
Rolled oats	2 cups	500 mL
All–purpose flour	1¼ cups	300 mL
Baking soda	1 tsp.	5 mL
Salt	½ tsp.	2 mL
Raisins	1 cup	250 mL

Cream butter, sugar and honey together well. Beat in egg and vanilla.

Add remaining ingredients. Mix well. Drop by spoonfuls onto greased baking sheet. Bake in 350°F (180°C) oven for 12 to 15 minutes. Makes 4 dozen.

Variation: Add 1 tbsp. (15 mL) grated orange rind.

Variation: Add 1 tbsp. (15 mL) cinnamon and 1 tbsp. (15 mL) grated lemon rind.

Pictured on page 89.

GRANOLA CHIPS

With cereal, raisins and rolled oats, this is a nutritious cookie.

Butter or margarine, softened	1 cup	250 mL
Granulated sugar	3/4 cup	175 mL
Brown sugar, packed	3/4 cup	175 mL
Eggs	2	2
Vanilla	1 tsp.	5 mL
All–purpose flour	1 1/2 cups	375 mL
Granola	2 cups	500 mL
Rolled oats	1 cup	250 mL
Baking powder	1 tsp.	5 mL
Salt	1/4 tsp.	1 mL
Raisins	1 cup	250 mL
Semisweet chocolate chips	1 cup	250 mL

Cream butter and both sugars together well. Beat in eggs 1 at a time. Add vanilla.

Add remaining ingredients. Stir. Drop by spoonfuls onto greased cookie sheet. Bake in 350°F (180°C) oven for 10 to 12 minutes. Makes 7 dozen.

Pictured on page 35.

MERINGUES

Food for the angels. Shattery–crisp with chocolate chips added.

Egg whites	2	2
Cream of tartar	1/4 tsp.	1 mL
Vanilla	1 tsp.	5 mL
Granulated sugar	3/4 cup	175 mL
Semisweet chocolate chips	1 cup	250 mL
Chopped pecans or walnuts	1 cup	250 mL

Beat egg whites, cream of tartar and vanilla together until soft peaks form.

Add sugar gradually beating until stiff.

Fold in chocolate chips and pecans. Drop by teaspoonfuls onto greased cookie sheet. Bake in 300°F (150°C) oven for 15 to 20 min–utes. Makes 2 1/2 dozen.

Pictured on page 143.

CHOCOLATE CHIPPERS

These chocolate chip cookies are tops. A drop cookie that doesn't flatten too much.

Butter or margarine, softened	1 cup	250 mL
Brown sugar, packed	1½ cups	375 mL
Eggs	2	2
Vanilla	1 tsp.	5 mL
All–purpose flour	2 cups	500 mL
Cornstarch	¼ cup	60 mL
Salt	¾ tsp.	4 mL
Baking soda	1 tsp.	5 mL
Semisweet chocolate chips	2 cups	500 mL
Chopped walnuts (optional)	1 cup	250 mL

Cream butter and sugar together. Beat in eggs 1 at a time. Add vanilla.

Stir flour, cornstarch, salt and baking soda together and add. Stir in chips and nuts. Drop by spoonfuls onto greased baking sheet. Bake in 350°F (180°C) oven for 10 to 15 minutes. Makes 5½ dozen.

Pictured on page 35.

CHOCOLATE DROPS

A soft, dark cookie.

Butter or margarine, softened	½ cup	125 mL
Granulated sugar	1 cup	250 mL
Egg	1	1
Cocoa	½ cup	125 mL
Milk	¼ cup	50 mL
Vanilla	1 tsp.	5 mL
All–purpose flour	1¾ cups	400 mL
Baking powder	1 tsp.	5 mL
Salt	½ tsp.	2 mL
Chopped nuts (optional)	½ cup	125 mL

Cream butter and sugar together. Beat in egg. Stir in cocoa, milk and vanilla.

Stir flour, baking powder and salt together and add along with nuts. Mix well. Drop by spoonfuls onto greased pan. Bake in 375°F (190°C) oven for 10 to 12 minutes. Makes 5 dozen.

Pictured on page 143.

FROG EYES

A good butter cookie that is colorful — eaten by young or old.

Butter or margarine, softened	1 cup	250 mL
Brown sugar, packed	1 cup	250 mL
Granulated sugar	½ cup	125 mL
Eggs	2	2
Vanilla	2 tsp.	10 mL
All–purpose flour	2¼ cups	550 mL
Baking soda	1 tsp.	5 mL
Salt	1 tsp.	5 mL
Candy–coated chocolate bits, such as Smarties or M & M's	½ cup	125 mL
Candy–coated chocolate bits, such as Smarties or M & M's	1 cup	250 mL

Cream butter and both sugars together. Beat in eggs 1 at a time. Mix in vanilla.

Add flour, baking soda, salt and first amount of chocolate bits. Mix well. Drop by spoonfuls onto ungreased cookie sheet.

Press remaining candies on top of cookies using 2 or 3 per cookie. Bake in 375°F (190°C) oven for 8 to 10 minutes until golden brown. Makes 4 dozen.

Pictured on page 35.

Paré Pointer

A karate school is one place where you don't knock before entering.

BEST DROP COOKIES

Good natural flavor with no spices added. Extra good.

Butter or margarine, softened	1 cup	250 mL
Brown sugar, packed	1½ cups	375 mL
Eggs	2	2
Vanilla	1 tsp.	5 mL
Dates, cut up	1 lb.	450 g
All–purpose flour	2 cups	450 mL
Rolled oats	1 cup	250 mL
Coconut	½ cup	125 mL
Baking soda	1 tsp.	5 mL
Chopped walnuts	½ cup	125 mL
Candied cherries, quartered, for color (optional)	½ cup	125 mL

Cream butter and sugar well. Beat in eggs and vanilla.

Add remaining ingredients. Mix well. Drop by spoonfuls onto greased baking sheet. Bake in 350°F (180°C) oven for 10 to 12 minutes. Makes 5 dozen.

Pictured on page 71.

SOFT MOLASSES DROPS

An old time recipe, these are moist and spicy.

All–purpose flour	3½ cups	800 mL
Granulated sugar	¾ cup	175 mL
Ginger	1 tsp.	5 mL
Cinnamon	1 tsp.	5 mL
Salt	½ tsp.	2 mL
Molasses	¾ cup	175 mL
Butter or margarine, softened	¾ cup	175 mL
Egg	1	1
Baking soda	1½ tsp.	7 mL
Hot coffee (or hot milk)	½ cup	125 mL

Measure first 8 ingredients in order given into mixing bowl.

Stir baking soda into hot coffee. Add and beat dough until thoroughly blended. Drop by tablespoons onto greased cookie sheet. Bake in 375°F (190°C) oven for 10 to 12 minutes. Makes 5 dozen.

Pictured on page 89.

OATMEAL MOLASSES COOKIES

Rich and chewy.

All-purpose flour	1½ cups	375 mL
Granulated sugar	½ cup	125 mL
Brown sugar	½ cup	125 mL
Baking soda	1 tsp.	5 mL
Salt	½ tsp.	2 mL
Ginger	½ tsp.	2 mL
Cloves	¼ tsp.	1 mL
Butter or margarine, softened	¾ cup	175 mL
Molasses	¼ cup	60 mL
Egg	1	1
Rolled oats	¾ cup	175 mL

Measure all ingredients, except rolled oats, in order given into mixing bowl. Beat well.

Stir in rolled oats. Drop by spoonfuls onto greased baking sheet. Bake in 375°F (190°C) oven for 8 to 10 minutes until browned. Makes 32 large cookies.

Pictured on page 125.

FRUIT COCKTAIL COOKIES

Probably this is the softest of all fruit cookies.

Butter or margarine, softened	½ cup	125 mL
Granulated sugar	½ cup	125 mL
Egg	1	1
Vanilla	½ tsp.	2 mL
Fruit cocktail, drained	14 oz.	398 mL
All-purpose flour	2 cups	500 mL
Baking soda	1 tsp.	5 mL
Salt	½ tsp.	2 mL
Cinnamon	½ tsp.	2 mL
Raisins	½ cup	125 mL
Chopped walnuts	½ cup	125 mL

Cream butter and sugar together. Beat in egg and vanilla. Stir in fruit.

Add remaining ingredients. Stir together. Drop by spoonfuls onto greased baking sheet. Bake in 350°F (180°C) oven until golden, about 10 minutes. Makes 4 dozen.

Pictured on page 89.

OATMEAL CHIP COOKIES

Chocolate chips in a favorite oatmeal base produce the ultimate cookie. A great favorite.

Butter or margarine, softened	1 cup	250 mL
Brown sugar, packed	2 cups	500 mL
Eggs	2	2
Vanilla	1 tsp.	5 mL
All–purpose flour	2 cups	500 mL
Baking powder	1 tsp.	5 mL
Baking soda	½ tsp.	2 mL
Rolled oats	2 cups	500 mL
Semisweet chocolate chips	2 cups	500 mL
Medium coconut	¾ cup	175 mL

Cream butter and sugar together. Beat in eggs 1 at a time. Add vanilla.

Add remaining ingredients. Mix well. Drop by spoonfuls onto greased baking sheet. Bake in 350°F (180°C) oven for about 8 to 10 minutes. Makes 5 dozen.

OATMEAL CHIP PIZZA: Press 3 cups (750 mL) dough into greased 12 inch (30 cm) pizza pan. Sprinkle with semisweet and butterscotch chips, nuts, coconut, candy coated chocolate (Smarties, M & M's), and any other treat you like. Allow a bit more time to bake.

Pictured on page 71.

Paré Pointer

The little firefly didn't stay because when you've got to glow, you've got to glow.

CHERRY COCONUT DROPS

This is golden brown with a light center. There is a subtle lemon flavor with cherries adding greatly to the festive look.

Butter or margarine, softened	1 cup	250 mL
Granulated sugar	1 cup	250 mL
Eggs	3	3
Sour cream	½ cup	125 mL
Lemon flavoring	1½ tsp.	7 mL
Grated orange rind	1 tsp.	5 mL
All–purpose flour	3¼ cups	800 mL
Baking powder	1 tsp.	5 mL
Baking soda	½ tsp.	2 mL
Salt	1 tsp.	5 mL
Chopped candied cherries	½ cup	125 mL
Shredded coconut	1 cup	250 mL

Cream butter and sugar together. Beat in eggs 1 at a time. Add sour cream, lemon flavoring and orange rind.

Mix in remaining ingredients in order given. Drop from teaspoon onto greased cookie sheet. Bake in 400°F (200°C) oven for 8 to 12 minutes. Makes about 6 dozen.

Pictured on page 17.

COCONUT CRUMB COOKIES

Bread crumbs replace flour in these but no one would ever guess.

Eggs	2	2
Granulated sugar (or brown)	1 cup	225 mL
Coconut	1 cup	225 mL
Dry bread crumbs	1 cup	225 mL

Beat eggs until frothy.

Stir in sugar, coconut and crumbs. Drop by spoonfuls onto greased baking sheet. Batter will be stiff. You may have to shape drops a bit with your hand. Bake in 350°F (180°C) oven until browned, 10 to 15 minutes. Makes 2½ dozen.

Pictured on page 71.

BROWN SUGAR COOKIES

Economical as well as good. Nuts may be added or not as wished.

Butter or margarine, softened	1 cup	250 mL
Brown sugar, packed	1 cup	250 mL
Egg	1	1
Vanilla	1 tsp.	5 mL
All–purpose flour	2 cups	500 mL
Baking soda	1 tsp.	5 mL
Salt	1/8 tsp.	0.5 mL

Cream butter and sugar together well. Beat in egg and vanilla.

Stir flour, soda and salt together and add. Mix well. Drop by teaspoon–fuls onto greased cookie sheet. Bake in 350°F (180°C) oven for 6 to 8 minutes. Makes 4 dozen.

Pictured on page 71.

RAGGED ROBINS

Quick and easy. Just combine beaten egg whites with other ingre–dients.

Egg whites, room temperature	2	2
Granulated sugar	1/2 cup	125 mL
Vanilla	1 tsp.	5 mL
Chopped dates	1 cup	250 mL
Chopped nuts	1 cup	250 mL
Cornflakes	2 cups	500 mL
Candied chopped cherries	1/4 cup	60 mL

Beat egg whites until soft peaks form. Gradually beat in sugar until stiff. Add vanilla.

Fold in dates, nuts, cornflakes and cherries. Drop by spoonfuls onto greased baking sheet. Bake in 325°F (160°C) oven for about 15 minutes. Makes 3 dozen.

Pictured on page 35.

BOILED RAISIN COOKIES

Spicy and moist, this is a different method of making good drop cookies.

Raisins	**2 cups**	**500 mL**
Water	**1 cup**	**250 mL**
Butter or margarine, softened	**1 cup**	**250 mL**
Brown sugar, packed	**1 cup**	**250 mL**
Granulated sugar	**1 cup**	**250 mL**
Eggs	**2**	**2**
All–purpose flour	**3 cups**	**750 mL**
Baking soda	**1 tsp.**	**5 mL**
Salt	**¾ tsp.**	**4 mL**
Cinnamon	**1¼ tsp.**	**6 mL**
Nutmeg	**½ tsp.**	**2 mL**
Allspice	**¼ tsp.**	**1 mL**
Rolled oats	**2 cups**	**500 mL**
Chopped nuts	**½ cup**	**125 mL**

Bring raisins and water to a boil in small saucepan. Boil 5 minutes. Cool.

Cream butter and both sugars together. Beat in eggs 1 at a time.

Stir remaining ingredients together and add to creamed mixture. Pour in raisins and juice. Mix well. Drop by spoonfuls onto greased baking sheet. Bake in 350°F (180°C) oven for 12 to 15 minutes. Makes 6 dozen.

Pictured on page 89.

Paré Pointer

The clock was removed from the library. It tocked too much.

DATE NUT COOKIES

This presents dates in a tasty, moist cookie.

Butter or margarine, softened	1 cup	250 mL
Granulated sugar	1 cup	250 mL
Eggs	3	3
Vanilla	1 tsp.	5 mL
All–purpose flour	2 cups	500 mL
Baking soda	1 tsp.	5 mL
Salt	½ tsp.	2 mL
Chopped dates	1 lb.	450 g
Chopped walnuts	1 cup	250 mL

Cream butter and sugar together. Beat in eggs 1 at a time. Add vanilla.

Mix in remaining ingredients. Drop by spoonfuls onto greased cookie sheet. Bake in 350°F (180°C) oven for 10 to 12 minutes. Makes 6 dozen.

Pictured on page 53.

PRALINE LACE

These look similar to Lace Cookies, page 46, however they contain no eggs or rolled oats.

Corn syrup	⅔ cup	150 mL
Butter or margarine, softened	⅔ cup	150 mL
Brown sugar, packed	⅔ cup	150 mL
All–purpose flour	1 cup	250 mL
Ground almonds	1 cup	250 mL

Combine syrup, butter and sugar in saucepan. Bring to a boil while stirring continually over medium heat. Remove from heat.

Stir in flour and almonds. Drop in scant 1 tsp. (5 mL) amounts onto greased cookie sheet. Bake in 375°F (190°C) oven for 4 to 5 minutes until edges brown. Let stand on pan for about 2 minutes before removing. Makes 5 dozen.

Pictured on page 143.

FILBERT FINGERS

Dainty and elegant describe these scrumptious cookies. Pretty as a picture.

Butter (not margarine) softened	1 cup	250 mL
Brown sugar, packed	¾ cup	175 mL
All–purpose flour	2½ cups	625 mL
Milk	2 tbsp.	30 mL
Ground filberts	1 cup	250 mL
Semi–sweet chocolate squares	2 x 1 oz.	2 x 28 g
Grated parowax (paraffin)	2 tbsp.	30 mL

Mix butter, sugar, flour and milk together. Form into a ball and knead until soft and pliable.

Mix in nuts. Shape into fingers. Place on ungreased baking sheet. Bake in 375°F (190°C) oven for about 10 minutes. Cool.

Melt chocolate and parowax in saucepan over hot water. Dip ends of fingers. Place on waxed paper to set. Makes 6½ dozen.

Pictured on page 143.

CAKE MIX COOKIES

Made from a cake mix from the shelf. Actually like a peanut butter cookie.

Smooth peanut butter	1 cup	250 mL
Butter or margarine, softened	¼ cup	60 mL
Water	¼ cup	60 mL
Eggs	2	2
Yellow cake mix, 2 layer size	1	1

Combine peanut butter, butter, water and eggs in bowl. Mix together.

Add cake mix. Stir well. Drop by teaspoonfuls onto ungreased cookie sheet. Press with floured fork in criss–cross style to flatten. Bake in 375°F (190°C) oven for about 10 minutes. Makes about 4 dozen.

Pictured on page 35.

OATMEAL RAISIN COOKIES

A moist drop type cookie.

Butter or margarine, softened	1 cup	250 mL
Brown sugar, packed	1 cup	250 mL
Egg	1	1
Vanilla	1 tsp.	5 mL
All–purpose flour	1½ cups	375 mL
Baking soda	1 tsp.	5 mL
Salt	¼ tsp.	1 mL
Rolled oats	1¼ cups	300 mL
Raisins	1 cup	250 mL

Cream butter and sugar together. Beat in egg and vanilla.

Add remaining ingredients. Mix well. Drop by spoonfuls onto greased cookie sheet. Bake in 350°F (180°C) oven for 8 to 10 minutes. Makes 3½ dozen.

Pictured on page 53.

FRUIT DROPS

These light–colored cookies are flavored with raisins, cherries and coconut. No spices in these.

Butter or margarine, softened	1 cup	250 mL
Brown sugar, packed	¾ cup	175 mL
Egg	1	1
Vanilla	1 tsp.	5 mL
Maraschino cherry juice	2 tbsp.	30 mL
All–purpose flour	2 cups	500 mL
Baking powder	½ tsp.	2 mL
Salt	¼ tsp.	1 mL
Raisins or currants	½ cup	125 mL
Chopped dates	½ cup	125 mL
Maraschino cherries, quartered	½ cup	125 mL
Shredded coconut	½ cup	125 mL

Cream butter and sugar well. Beat in egg, vanilla and cherry juice.

Measure in remaining ingredients. Stir to mix. Drop by spoonfuls onto greased cookie sheet. Bake in 375°F (190°C) oven for 10 to 12 min–utes. Makes 3½ dozen.

Pictured on page 17.

SPICY DADS

A spicy version of the commercial variety.

Butter or margarine, softened	1 cup	250 mL
Granulated sugar	1 cup	250 mL
Brown sugar, packed	½ cup	125 mL
Egg	1	1
Molasses	2 tbsp.	30 mL
Vanilla	1 tsp.	5 mL
All–purpose flour	1½ cups	375 mL
Rolled oats	1½ cups	375 mL
Coconut	1 cup	250 mL
Baking powder	1 tsp.	5 mL
Baking soda	1 tsp.	5 mL
Cinnamon	1 tsp.	5 mL
Nutmeg	1 tsp.	5 mL
Allspice	1 tsp.	5 mL

Cream butter and both sugars together. Beat in egg. Add molasses and vanilla.

Stir remaining ingredients together and add. Mix well. Drop by spoon–fuls onto greased baking sheet. Press with floured fork. Bake in 300°F (150°C) oven until golden, about 12 minutes. Makes 6 dozen.

Pictured on page 71.

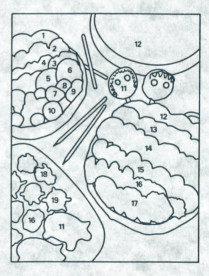

LEMONADE COOKIES

Made with concentrated lemonade, these are soft and moist with just a hint of lemon.

Butter or margarine, softened	1 cup	250 mL
Granulated sugar	1 cup	250 mL
Eggs	2	2
Frozen concentrated lemonade, thawed and halved	6 oz.	170 mL
All–purpose flour	3 cups	750 mL
Baking soda	1 tsp.	5 mL
Salt	½ tsp.	2 mL

Concentrated lemonade for garnish

Cream butter and sugar together. Beat in eggs 1 at a time. Add 3 oz. (85 mL) concentrated lemonade.

Stir flour, baking soda and salt together and add. Mix well. Drop by spoonfuls onto greased cookie sheet. Bake in 375°F (190°C) oven for 10 to 12 minutes until light brown.

Brush tops of cookies with concentrated lemonade. Makes about 5 dozen.

Note: If frozen concentrated lemonade is not available, stir ½ cup (125 mL) hot water with ¼ cup (60 mL) lemon juice and ¼ cup (60 mL) granulated sugar until mixed and sugar is dissolved. Use as directed above.

Pictured on page 35.

DATE MERINGUES

These actually melt in your mouth.

Egg whites, room temperature	2	2
Icing (confectioner's) sugar	1 cup	250 mL
Chopped dates	1 cup	250 mL

In mixing bowl beat egg whites until soft peaks form. Add sugar gradually continuing to beat until stiff. Fold in dates. Drop by spoon–fuls onto greased cookie sheet. Bake in 300°F (150°C) oven for about 12 to 15 minutes. Makes 2 dozen.

Pictured on page 143.

BRAN CEREAL COOKIES

These chewy cookies are good with or without cinnamon.

Butter or margarine, softened	1 cup	250 mL
Granulated sugar	1 cup	250 mL
Eggs	2	2
Vanilla	1½ tsp.	7 mL
All-purpose flour	1½ cups	375 mL
Baking soda	1 tsp.	5 mL
Salt	½ tsp.	2 mL
Cinnamon (optional)	1 tsp.	5 mL
All bran cereal	1½ cups	375 mL
Chopped nuts	1 cup	250 mL

Cream butter and sugar together. Beat in eggs 1 at a time. Add vanilla.

Measure in remaining ingredients. Mix well. Drop by spoonfuls onto greased baking sheet. Bake in 375°F (190°C) oven for 12 to 14 minutes. Makes 4 dozen.

Pictured on page 35.

CHOCOLATE NUGGETS

These are incredible cookies. They are extra rich and extra chocolaty and brownie-like. Make for a special treat when cost is no object.

Semisweet chocolate chips	2 cups	500 mL
Butter or margarine	¼ cup	60 mL
Sweetened condensed milk	11 oz.	300 mL
Granulated sugar	¼ cup	60 mL
Vanilla	1 tsp.	5 mL
All-purpose flour	1 cup	250 mL
Chopped nuts (optional)	½ cup	125 mL

Melt first 5 ingredients together in saucepan over medium heat. Stir often.

Add flour and nuts. Mix well. Drop by spoonfuls onto greased cookie sheet. Bake in 350°F (180°C) oven for about 10 to 12 minutes. Cookies will be soft. Makes 6 dozen.

Pictured on page 143.

So caramelly tasting. A great cookie jar type.

Eggs	2	2
Brown sugar, packed	1 cup	250 mL
Granulated sugar	½ cup	125 mL
Cooking oil	1 cup	250 mL
Vanilla	1 tsp.	5 mL
Baking soda	1 tsp.	5 mL
Hot water	1 tbsp.	15 mL
Rolled oats	2 cups	500 mL
All–purpose flour	1½ cups	375 mL
Salt	1 tsp.	5 mL

Beat eggs in mixing bowl until frothy. Beat in both sugars. Add cooking oil and vanilla.

Dissolve baking soda in hot water. Stir in.

Add oats, flour and salt. Stir well. Drop by spoonfuls onto greased baking sheet. Bake in 350°F (180°C) oven for about 8 minutes. Makes 3½ dozen. To make lollipops see page 92.

RAISIN OATMEAL: Add 1 cup (250 mL) raisins. If you would like spice too, add 1 tsp. (5 mL) cinnamon, ¼ tsp. (1 mL) nutmeg and ¼ tsp. (1 mL) allspice. Nuts are optional, ½ cup (125 mL).

Pictured on page 71.

LOLLIPOPS: To make oatmeal lollipops see method in Rolled Ginger Cookies recipe on page 93.

PEANUT CEREAL STACKS

Quick to prepare this firm, chewy cookie.

Smooth peanut butter	½ cup	125 mL
Granulated sugar	½ cup	125 mL
Evaporated milk	¼ cup	60 mL
Cornflakes	2½ cups	625 mL

Put peanut butter, sugar and milk into bowl. Blend together until smooth. Add cornflakes. Mix well to coat evenly. Drop by teaspoonfuls onto ungreased cookie sheet. Bake in 375°F (190°C) oven until browned, about 6 minutes. Makes about 2½ dozen.

Pictured on page 89.

CHOCOLATE CREAM DROPS

A very mellow chocolate flavor. Tops.

Butter or margarine, softened	1 cup	250 mL
Cream cheese, softened	4 oz.	125 g
Granulated sugar	1½ cups	375 mL
Egg	1	1
Milk	2 tbsp.	30 mL
Vanilla	½ tsp.	2 mL
Unsweetened chocolate squares, melted	2 x 1 oz.	2 x 28 g
Cake flour	2½ cups	600 mL
Baking powder	1½ tsp.	7 mL
Salt	¼ tsp.	1 mL
Chopped walnuts	½ cup	125 mL

Cream butter, cheese and sugar together well. Beat in egg, milk, vanilla and chocolate.

Stir remaining ingredients together and add. Mix well. Drop by spoon–fuls onto greased baking sheet. Bake in 350°F (180°C) oven for 10 to 12 minutes. To have a continuing supply of these, pack in layers in plastic container while still a bit warm, with plastic wrap in between layers. Cover with lid and freeze. When removed to serve, they are moist and luscious. Makes 5 dozen.

Pictured on page 89.

PINEAPPLE COOKIES

A refreshing fruity flavor.

Butter or margarine, softened	½ cup	125 mL
Granulated sugar	½ cup	125 mL
Egg	1	1
Vanilla	1 tsp.	5 mL
Crushed pineapple, drained	½ cup	125 ml
All–purpose flour	2 cups	500 mL
Baking powder	1 tsp.	5 mL
Baking soda	1 tsp.	5 mL
Salt	½ tsp.	2 mL
Granulated sugar	1 tbsp.	15 mL
Nutmeg	¼ tsp.	1 mL

(continued on next page)

Cream butter and first amount of sugar together well. Beat in egg. Stir in vanilla and pineapple.

Add flour, baking powder, soda and salt. Stir. Drop by spoonfuls onto ungreased baking sheet.

Mix second amount of sugar and nutmeg together. Sprinkle on top of unbaked cookies. Bake in 375°F (190°C) oven for about 8 to 10 minutes. Makes about 3 dozen.

Pictured on page 53.

FRUIT JUMBLES

A fruity spice–colored cookie. Makes a batch large enough to exchange with friends.

Candied cherries, chopped	1 cup	250 mL
Chopped dates	1 cup	250 mL
Chopped nuts	1 cup	250 mL
Raisins	1 cup	250 mL
Cut mixed peel	1/4 cup	60 mL
All–purpose flour	1/2 cup	125 mL
Butter or margarine, softened	1 1/2 cups	350 mL
Brown sugar, packed	1 cup	250 mL
Granulated sugar	1 cup	250 mL
Eggs	3	3
All–purpose flour	3 1/2 cups	800 mL
Baking powder	1 tsp.	5 mL
Baking soda	1 tsp.	5 mL
Salt	1 tsp.	5 mL
Cinnamon	1 tsp.	5 mL
Cloves	1/8 tsp.	0.5 mL

Measure first 6 ingredients into bowl. Mix thoroughly.

In another bowl cream butter and both sugars together. Add eggs 1 at a time, beating after each addition.

Stir remaining ingredients together. Add and mix well. Add fruit. Mix together. Drop by spoonfuls onto greased baking sheet. Bake in 375°F (190°C) oven for 8 to 10 minutes. Makes 10 dozen.

Pictured on page 53.

CARROT COOKIES

A moist cookie that uses leftover or fresh carrots. These contain rolled oats.

Butter or margarine, softened	½ cup	125 mL
Granulated sugar	1 cup	250 mL
Egg	1	1
Cooked, mashed carrots (or fresh, grated)	1 cup	250 mL
Milk	⅓ cup	75 mL
Vanilla	1 tsp.	5 mL
All–purpose flour	2 cups	500 mL
Rolled oats	2 cups	500 mL
Baking powder	2 tsp.	10 mL
Salt	¼ tsp.	1 mL
Cinnamon	1 tsp.	5 mL
Raisins	1 cup	250 mL

Cream butter and sugar well. Beat in egg. Mix in carrot, milk and vanilla.

Add remaining ingredients. Mix well. Drop by spoonfuls onto greased cookie sheet. Bake in 375°F (190°C) oven for about 12 to 15 minutes until slightly browned. Frost if desired. Makes about 4 dozen.

ICING

Icing (confectioner's) sugar	2½ cups	625 mL
Butter or margarine, softened	⅓ cup	75 mL
Prepared orange juice	2–3 tbsp.	30–50 mL
Grated orange rind	1½ tbsp.	25 mL

Beat all together adding more or less orange juice to make icing proper consistency. Ice or dip cookies into icing.

Pictured on page 35.

Paré Pointer

You have to know all the angles to pass a geometry test.

CHRISTMAS COOKIES

These are moist with a Brazil nut flavor. An attractive cookie.

Butter or margarine, softened	1 cup	250 mL
Brown sugar, packed	3/4 cup	175 mL
Egg	1	1
All–purpose flour	1 1/4 cups	300 mL
Salt	1/2 tsp.	2 mL
Cinnamon	1/2 tsp.	2 mL
Baking soda	1/2 tsp.	2 mL
Chopped dates	1/2 cup	125 mL
Glazed cherries, chopped	1/2 cup	125 mL
Candied pineapple slices, chopped	2	2
Chopped walnuts	1 cup	250 mL
Slivered almonds	1/2 cup	125 mL
Brazil nuts, chopped	1/2 cup	125 mL

Cream butter and sugar together. Beat in egg.

Stir flour, salt, cinnamon and baking soda together and add. Mix to combine.

Add remaining ingredients. Mix well. Drop by spoonfuls onto greased cookie sheet. Bake in 350°F (180°C) oven for 10 to 15 minutes. Makes 5 dozen.

Pictured on page 17.

CORNFLAKE MACAROONS

These are both crispy and chewy.

Egg whites, room temperature	2	2
Granulated sugar	3/4 cup	175 mL
Vanilla	1/2 tsp.	2 mL
Cornflakes	2 cups	500 mL
Chopped nuts	1/2 cup	125 mL
Shredded coconut	1 cup	250 mL

In mixing bowl beat egg whites until soft peaks form. Add sugar gradually beating until stiff. Add vanilla.

Fold in cornflakes, nuts and coconut. Drop by spoonfuls onto greased baking sheet. Bake in 325°F (160°C) oven for 12 to 15 minutes. Makes 3 dozen.

Pictured on page 89.

GUM DROPS

These are extra chewy with gum drops baked in them.

Butter or margarine, softened	1 cup	250 mL
Brown sugar, packed	1 cup	250 mL
Granulated sugar	¼ cup	60 mL
Eggs	2	2
Vanilla	1 tsp.	5 mL
All–purpose flour	1½ cups	350 mL
Baking powder	1 tsp.	5 mL
Baking soda	½ tsp.	2 mL
Salt	½ tsp.	2 mL
Rolled oats	1 cup	250 mL
Gumdrops, cut up (no black)	1 cup	250 mL
Chopped nuts (optional)	½ cup	125 mL

Cream butter and both sugars together. Beat in eggs 1 at a time. Add vanilla.

Add remaining ingredients. Mix well. Drop by spoonfuls onto ungreased baking sheet. Bake in 350°F (180°C) oven for 12 to 14 minutes. Makes 4 dozen.

Pictured on cover.

ALMOND MACAROONS

A shattery good Italian treat.

Egg whites, room temperature	2	2
Granulated sugar	1 cup	250 mL
Ground almonds	1 cup	250 mL
Cornstarch	2 tbsp.	30 mL
Almond flavoring	¼ tsp.	1 mL
Maraschino cherries or almonds		

Beat egg whites until soft peaks form. Add sugar gradually, beating until stiff.

Fold in almonds, cornstarch and flavorings. Drop by spoonfuls onto greased baking sheet, flattening slightly with finger if needed.

(continued on next page)

Place whole or half cherry or almond in center. These are also good without cherries or almonds. Bake in 325°F (160°C) oven for about 15 minutes. Makes about 2½ dozen.

Pictured on page 17.

RAINBOW CHIP COOKIES

These delicious cookies contain no flour. Soft and chewy with candy–coated chocolate added. Makes a huge batch.

Smooth peanut butter	6 cups	1.3 L
Butter or margarine, softened	2 cups	500 mL
Brown sugar, packed	6 cups	1.3 L
Granulated sugar	4 cups	1 L
Eggs	12	12
Vanilla	1 tbsp.	15 mL
Corn syrup	1 tbsp.	15 mL
Rolled oats	18 cups	4 L
Baking soda	8 tsp.	40 mL
Semisweet chocoate chips	2 cups	450 mL
Candy–coated chocolate bits, such as Smarties or M & M's	2 cups	450 mL

In mixing bowl, cream peanut butter, butter, brown and granulated sugar together. Beat in eggs, 2 at a time. Mix in vanilla and syrup. Transfer to extra large container.

Mix in remaining ingredients. Drop by ice cream scoop onto greased pan. Flatten with hand. May be dropped by teaspoonfuls for a smaller cookie. Bake in 350° F (180° C) oven for 10 to 12 minutes for large cookies and 7 to 8 minutes for small. Overbaking makes them hard. Makes 5 dozen, 3 inch (8 cm) cookies, 1 dozen, 5 inch (13 cm) cookies and 1 pizza cookie.

PIZZA: Use 3 cups (700 mL) cookie dough. Press into 12 inch (30 cm) pizza pan. Sprinkle with more semisweet chocolate chips, but–terscotch chips, Smarties or M & M's, cereal flakes, coconut, peanuts and any other things you fancy. Bake for 12 to 15 minutes. Serve in wedges, warm or cold.

Pictured on page 35.

LACE COOKIES

When baked, these are full of holes giving them a lacy look. Fancy.

Butter or margarine, melted	³/₄ cup	175 mL
Granulated sugar	³/₄ cup	175 mL
Brown sugar, packed	³/₄ cup	175 mL
Egg	1	1
Vanilla	1 tsp.	5 mL
Rolled oats	1¹/₂ cups	375 mL
All–purpose flour	¹/₄ cup	60 mL
Baking powder	1 tsp.	5 mL
Salt	¹/₄ tsp.	1 mL

In mixing bowl beat butter and both sugars well. Beat in egg and vanilla.

Add remaining ingredients. Mix. Drop by ¹/₂ tsp. (2.5 mL) onto greased cookie sheet. Bake in 375°F (190°C) oven for about 4 minutes. Let stand 1 to 3 minutes before removing until they can be removed without tearing. Leave flat for a lacy appearance. Makes about 6¹/₂ dozen.

Pictured on page 143.

QUICK MACAROONS

Fast to make these chewy cookies. May be made with or without cherries.

Shredded coconut	2¹/₂ cups	625 mL
Sweetened condensed milk	¹/₂ cup	125 mL
Vanilla	1 tsp.	5 mL
Maraschino cherries	6–12	6–12

Put first 3 ingredients into bowl. Mix well. Drop by spoonfuls onto greased baking sheet about 1 inch (2.5 cm) apart.

Top with ¹/₄ or ¹/₂ maraschino cherry. Bake in 350°F (180°C) oven for 8 to 10 minutes. Remove immediately from baking sheet. Makes 2 dozen.

Pictured on page 17.

Raisins, currants, fruit and nuts combine to make fruited cookies instead of fruit cake.

Golden raisins	½ cup	125 mL
Currants or raisins	½ cup	125 mL
Candied cut mixed fruit	2 cups	500 mL
Chopped pecans or walnuts	1 cup	250 mL
All–purpose flour	½ cup	125 mL
Butter or margarine, softened	½ cup	125 mL
Granulated sugar	¾ cup	175 mL
Eggs	2	2
Vanilla	1 tsp.	5 mL
Brandy flavoring	2 tsp.	10 mL
All–purpose flour	1 cup	250 mL
Baking soda	1 tsp.	5 mL
Salt	¼ tsp.	1 mL
Cinnamon	½ tsp.	2 mL
Nutmeg	¼ tsp.	1 mL

Measure first 5 ingredients into bowl. Stir well to coat. Set aside.

Cream butter and sugar together. Beat in eggs 1 at a time. Add vanilla and brandy flavoring.

Stir remaining ingredients together and add. Mix in fruit. Drop by spoonfuls onto greased baking sheet. Bake in 325°F (190°C) oven for 15 to 20 minutes. Makes 5 dozen.

Pictured on page 17.

Paré Pointer

Did you know there are only twenty four letters in the alphabet? E.T. went home.

APPLE COOKIES

When these bake there is an aroma of apple pie. A soft drop–cookie.

Butter or margarine, softened	½ cup	125 mL
Brown sugar, packed	1½ cups	375 mL
Egg	1	1
All–purpose flour	2 cups	500 mL
Baking soda	1 tsp.	5 mL
Cinnamon	1 tsp.	5 mL
Cloves	½ tsp.	2 mL
Nutmeg	½ tsp.	2 mL
Salt	½ tsp.	2 mL
Apple, peeled and grated	1 cup	250 mL
Raisins	1 cup	250 mL
Chopped walnuts or pecans	1 cup	250 mL
Milk	¼ cup	60 mL

Put butter, sugar and egg into mixing bowl. Beat well until smooth.

Stir flour, baking soda, cinnamon, cloves, nutmeg and salt together and add. Mix.

Stir in remaining ingredients. Drop by teaspoonfuls onto greased baking sheet. Bake in 400°F (200°C) oven for 8 to 10 minutes. When cool spread with Caramel or Vanilla Icing. Makes 5 dozen.

CARAMEL ICING

Butter or margarine	2 tbsp.	30 mL
Brown sugar, packed	2 tbsp.	30 mL
Icing (confectioner's) sugar	¾ cup	175 mL
Milk	4 tsp.	20 mL

Combine butter and sugar in small saucepan. Stir and bring to boil over medium heat. Simmer 2 minutes. Remove from heat. Add icing sugar and milk. Add more milk or sugar if needed to make proper spreading consistency. Ice cookies.

(continued on next page)

VANILLA ICING

Icing (confectioner's) sugar	³/₄ cup	175 mL
Butter or margarine, softened	2 tsp.	10 mL
Vanilla	¹/₈ tsp.	0.5 mL
Milk	1 tbsp.	15 mL

Mix all together adding more milk if needed to make spreading con-sistency. Ice cookies.

Pictured on page 125.

CHOCOLATE SOFTIES

Jazz these up with a bit of icing.

Butter or margarine, softened	¹/₂ cup	125 mL
Granulated sugar	1 cup	250 mL
Egg	1	1
Squares of unsweetened chocolate, melted	2 x 1 oz.	2 x 28 g
Sour milk	¹/₃ cup	75 mL
Vanilla	1 tsp.	5 mL
All–purpose flour	1³/₄ cups	400 mL
Baking soda	¹/₂ tsp.	2 mL
Salt	¹/₂ tsp.	2 mL
Chopped walnuts (optional)	¹/₂ cup	125 mL

Mix first 6 ingredients together well.

Stir in remaining ingredients. Drop by teaspoonfuls onto ungreased cookie sheet, allowing room for spreading. Bake in 400°F (200°C) oven for about 8 to 10 minutes. When pressed slightly, it should leave no dent. Remove from cookie sheet. Cool. Makes 4 dozen.

ICING

Icing (confectioner's) sugar	1¹/₄ cups	300 mL
Cocoa	¹/₃ cup	75 mL
Butter or margarine, softened	3 tbsp.	45 mL
Hot coffee or water	5 tsp.	25 mL

Beat all together until smooth, adding a bit more liquid if needed to make proper spreading consistency. Ice cookies.

Pictured on cover.

ZUCCHINI DROPS

Little heaps of moist goodness. Lightly spiced.

Butter or margarine, softened	¾ cup	175 mL
Granulated sugar	1½ cups	375 mL
Eggs	2	2
Grated zucchini, unpeeled	1½ cups	375 mL
Vanilla	1 tsp.	5 mL
All–purpose flour	2½ cups	625 mL
Baking powder	1 tsp.	5 mL
Baking soda	1 tsp.	5 mL
Cinnamon	1½ tsp.	7 mL
Salt	½ tsp.	2 mL
Raisins	1½ cups	375 mL
Chopped walnuts	1 cup	250 mL

Cream butter and sugar well. Beat in eggs 1 at a time. Add zucchini and vanilla.

Stir remaining ingredients together and add. Mix well. Drop by spoon–fuls onto greased baking sheet. Bake in 350°F (180°C) oven for 12 to 15 minutes. Makes 5 dozen.

Pictured on page 89.

CARROT SPICE COOKIES

For a healthy variation, use whole wheat flour to replace half of the white.

Butter or margarine, softened	½ cup	125 mL
Brown sugar, packed	1 cup	250 mL
Egg	1	1
Grated carrot	1½ cups	375 mL
All–purpose flour or whole wheat	2 cups	500 mL
Baking powder	1 tsp.	5 mL
Baking soda	½ tsp.	2 mL
Salt	¼ tsp.	1 mL
Cinnamon	½ tsp.	2 mL

(continued on next page)

Cream butter and sugar well. Beat in egg. Stir in carrot.

Stir remaining ingredients together and add. Mix well. Drop by spoon-fuls onto greased cookie sheet. Bake in 350°F (180°C) oven for 10 to 12 minutes. Makes about 3 dozen.

Pictured on page 89.

THRESHER'S COOKIES

Ideal cookie jar filler–upper for after school or after work snacks.

Rolled oats	3 cups	750 mL
All–purpose flour	2½ cups	625 mL
Baking soda	1½ tsp.	8 mL
Cinnamon	1 tsp.	5 mL
Allspice	½ tsp.	2 mL
Salt	½ tsp.	2 mL
Raisins	1 cup	250 ml
Chopped walnuts	1 cup	250 mL
Currants	½ cup	125 mL
Coconut	½ cup	125 mL
Eggs	3	3
Granulated sugar	1½ cups	375 mL
Sour cream	2 cups	500 mL
Vanilla	1 tsp.	5 mL

Measure first 10 ingredients into large bowl. Mix well.

In second bowl, beat eggs until frothy. Add sugar, sour cream and vanilla. Pour into dry ingredients in first bowl. Mix well. Drop by spoonfuls onto greased cookie sheet. Bake in 350°F (180°C) oven for 10 to 15 minutes. Makes 8 dozen.

Pictured on page 71.

Paré Pointer

Two little birds were sent home from school. They were caught peep-ing during an exam.

BANANA DROPS

These are great with or without cinnamon.

Butter or margarine, softened	½ cup	125 mL
Granulated sugar	1 cup	250 mL
Eggs	2	2
Mashed banana	1 cup	250 mL
All–purpose flour	2 cups	500 mL
Baking powder	1 tbsp.	15 mL
Salt	¼ tsp.	1 mL
Chopped nuts	½ cup	125 mL
Raisins (optional)	1 cup	250 mL
Cinnamon (optional)	1 tsp.	5 mL

Cream butter and sugar together. Beat in eggs 1 at a time. Add banana.

Measure in remaining ingredients. Mix well. Drop by spoonfuls onto greased cookie sheet. Bake in 375°F (190°C) oven for 8 to 10 minutes. Makes 4 dozen.

Pictured on page 71.

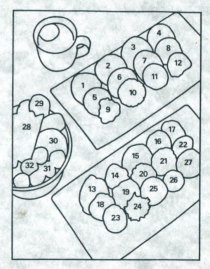

The grated orange rind gives these their distinctive flavor.

Eggs	2	2
Granulated sugar	1 cup	250 mL
Brown sugar, packed	½ cup	125 mL
Cooking oil	1 cup	250 mL
All–purpose flour	2 cups	500 mL
Baking powder	1 tsp.	5 mL
Baking soda	½ tsp.	2 mL
Salt	½ tsp.	2 mL
Cinnamon	1 tsp.	5 mL
Grated orange rind	1 tbsp.	15 mL
Prepared orange juice (or milk)	2 tbsp.	30 mL
Rolled oats	3 cups	750 mL

Beat eggs in mixing bowl until frothy. Beat in both sugars. Add cooking oil.

Stir next 5 ingredients together and add.

Add remaining ingredients. Mix well. Drop by spoonfuls onto greased cookie sheet. Bake in 350°F (180°C) oven for 10 to 12 minutes. Makes about 5 dozen.

Pictured on page 71.

Eve knew she wouldn't get the mumps because she'd Adam.

RAISIN BRAN COOKIES

This could even be a breakfast cookie.

Butter or margarine, softened	½ cup	125 mL
Brown sugar, packed	1 cup	250 mL
Egg	1	1
Vanilla	1 tsp.	5 mL
All–purpose flour	1 cup	250 mL
Baking powder	1 tsp.	5 mL
Cinnamon (optional)	1 tsp.	5 mL
Salt	½ tsp.	2 mL
Raisins (optional)	⅓ cup	75 mL
Chopped nuts	⅓ cup	75 mL
All bran cereal	½ cup	125 mL

Cream butter and sugar well. Beat in egg and vanilla.

Add remaining ingredients. Mix well. Drop by spoonfuls onto greased baking sheet. Flatten with wet fork. Bake in 350°F (180°C) oven for 10 to 12 minutes. Makes 3 dozen.

Pictured on page 53.

CHOCOLATE HERMITS

A favorite cookie with an irresistible chocolate flavor.

Unsweetened chocolate squares	6 x 1 oz.	6 x 28 g
Butter or margarine, softened	1 cup	250 mL
Granulated sugar	1 cup	250 mL
Brown sugar, packed	1 cup	250 mL
Eggs	2	2
Milk	¼ cup	60 mL
Vanilla	2 tsp.	10 mL
All–purpose flour	2¾ cups	650 mL
Baking powder	1 tbsp.	15 mL
Baking soda	1 tsp.	5 mL
Cinnamon	2 tsp.	10 mL
Raisins	1½ cups	375 mL
Chopped dates (optional)	¾ cup	175 mL
Chopped nuts	1¼ cups	300 mL

(continued on next page)

In small heavy saucepan melt chocolate over low heat. Set aside.

Cream butter and both sugars in mixing bowl. Beat in eggs 1 at a time. Add milk and vanilla. Stir. Add melted chocolate and mix well.

Stir flour, baking powder, baking soda and cinnamon together. Add to chocolate mixture. Mix well. Add raisins, dates and nuts. Stir. Drop by spoonfuls onto greased baking sheet. Bake in 350°F (180°C) oven for about 13 to 15 minutes. If these flatten too much during baking, chill cookies before placing in oven. Makes 4 dozen.

Pictured on page 35.

QUICK OATMEAL COOKIES

An easy way to make oatmeal cookies. Try these with date filling as well.

Rolled oats	3 cups	750 mL
Brown sugar, packed	1 cup	250 mL
All–purpose flour	1 cup	250 mL
Salt	1/2 tsp.	2 mL
Vanilla	1 tsp.	5 mL
Butter or margarine, melted	1 cup	250 mL
Boiling water	1/4 cup	60 mL
Baking soda	1 tsp.	5 mL

Measure first 6 ingredients into mixing bowl. Mix together well.

Stir water and baking soda together. Add. Mix well. Shape into 2 inch (5 cm) rolls. Wrap and chill. Dough may also be frozen. When ready to bake slice thinly. Place on ungreased pan. Bake in 375°F (190°C) oven for 8 to 10 minutes. Makes 4 dozen.

QUICK DATE FILLED COOKIES: Use Date Filling, page 94, to sand–wich these cookies together. Saves rolling the dough. Excellent.

Pictured on pages 89 and 125.

SHORTBREAD

So delicate! Keep a supply in the freezer. It thaws quickly.

Butter (not margarine), softened	1 lb.	454 g
Sugar, use half brown and half icing (confectioner's)	¾ cup	175 mL
All–purpose flour	4 cups	900 mL

Red and green sugar, mixed
Candied cherries, cut up

Mix butter, sugar and flour together well. With your hands, squeeze and work until it will hold together. Make 4 rolls about 1½ inches (3.5 cm) in diameter. May be sliced and baked at this point but makes a much rounder cookie if chilled first. May be chilled overnight or just an hour or two. Slice ¼ inch (1.1 cm) thick. Arrange on ungreased baking sheet.

Sprinkle some cookies with sugar. Lightly push piece of cherry into center of some others. Bake at 325°F (160°C) oven for about 15 to 20 minutes or until lightly browned around edges. Remove from baking sheet to counter top. Makes about 6 dozen.

Note: For a whiter shortbread use all icing sugar instead of part brown sugar. May also be rolled on lightly floured surface and cut into shapes.

Pictured on page 17.

ICE BOX BRAN COOKIES

Crunchy good. Keep dough in refrigerator or freezer.

Butter or margarine, softened	1½ cups	375 mL
Brown sugar, packed	2 cups	500 mL
Eggs	2	2
All–purpose flour	3 cups	750 mL
All bran cereal	1 cup	250 mL
Baking powder	2 tsp.	10 mL

Cream butter and sugar together. Beat in eggs 1 at a time.

Stir in flour, cereal and baking powder. Shape into 2 inch (5 cm) rolls. Wrap and chill overnight. Next day slice thinly and arrange on ungreased baking sheet. Any unused dough may be frozen. Bake in 400°F (200°C) oven for about 8 minutes. Makes 6 dozen.

Pictured on page 89.

CHRISTMAS ICE BOX COOKIES

Good any other time as well. Pretty on a plate of goodies.

Butter or margarine, softened	1 cup	250 mL
Brown sugar, packed	1½ cups	375 mL
Eggs	2	2
Vanilla	1 tsp.	5 mL
All–purpose flour	3½ cups	875 mL
Baking soda	1 tsp.	5 mL
Salt	¼ tsp.	1 mL
Candied cherries, quartered	¾ cup	175 mL
Finely chopped nuts	½ cup	125 mL
Currants (optional)	½ cup	125 mL

In mixing bowl cream butter and sugar together. Beat in eggs 1 at a time. Add vanilla.

Stir flour, baking soda and salt together and mix in. Add cherries, nuts and currants. Mix and shape into round or square logs approximately 2 inches (5 cm) in diameter. Wrap and chill overnight or longer. May be frozen also. When ready to bake slice thinly. Arrange on ungreased baking sheet. Bake in 375°F (190°C) oven for 6 to 7 minutes until very light brown.

Pictured on page 17.

CREAM CHEESE COOKIES

These little rounds are topped with jam and baked. Some are rolled.

Butter or margarine, softened	½ cup	125 mL
Cream cheese, softened	2 oz.	60 g
Granulated sugar	⅓ cup	75 mL
Vanilla	½ tsp.	2 mL
All–purpose flour	1 cup	250 mL

Jam, red or orange

Mix first five ingredients together. Shape into rolls. Wrap and chill overnight. Dough may be frozen.

When ready to bake, slice thinly. Put dab of jam on some and place on ungreased baking sheet. Put dab of jam on others and roll. Place these on greased baking sheet. Bake in 350°F (180°C) oven for about 10 minutes until golden brown. Makes 3 dozen.

Pictured on page 17.

CHOCOLATE ICE BOX COOKIES

Dark and delicious. For a solid chocolate appearance, simply omit the nuts or roll logs in nuts before chilling.

Butter or margarine, softened	³/₄ cup	175 mL
Granulated sugar	1 cup	250 mL
Egg	1	1
Vanilla	1 tsp.	5 mL
Unsweetened chocolate squares, melted	3 x 1 oz.	3 x 28 g
All–purpose flour	2¹/₂ cups	625 mL
Baking powder	1¹/₂ tsp.	7 mL
Salt	¹/₂ tsp.	2 mL
Finely chopped pecans or walnuts	1 cup	250 mL

Cream butter and sugar together. Beat in egg, vanilla and melted chocolate.

Add remaining ingredients. Mix together. Shape into rolls 2 inches (5 cm) in diameter or oblongs 1 x 2 inches (2.5 x 5 cm). Wrap in waxed paper or plastic. Chill overnight or longer. May also be frozen. To bake, slice thinly and place on ungreased cookie sheet. Bake in 375°F (190°C) oven for about 5 minutes. Makes 8 to 9 dozen.

Pictured on page 17.

VANILLA WAFERS

For a variation, add one tablespoon (fifteen milliliters) powdered instant coffee granules to make coffee wafers.

Butter or margarine, softened	¹/₂ cup	125 mL
Granulated sugar	³/₄ cup	175 mL
Egg	1	1
Corn syrup	2 tbsp.	30 mL
Vanilla	1 tsp.	5 mL
Baking soda	2 tsp.	10 mL
Hot water	1 tbsp.	15 mL
All–purpose flour	2¹/₃ cups	575 mL

Cream butter and sugar together. Beat in egg, syrup, and vanilla.

Dissolve baking soda in water. Add.

Mix in flour. Shape into 2 inch (5 cm) rolls. Wrap and chill overnight or longer. Slice thinly and place on ungreased cookie sheet. Bake in 400°F (200°C) oven for 6 to 8 minutes. Makes about 8 dozen.

Pictured on page 125.

SPICED ICE BOX COOKIES

These are spicy, crisp and good keepers.

Butter or margarine, softened	1 cup	250 mL
Brown sugar, packed	2/3 cup	150 mL
Granulated sugar	2/3 cup	150 mL
Eggs	2	2
Vanilla	1 tsp.	5 mL
All–purpose flour	3 cups	750 mL
Baking soda	1 tsp.	5 mL
Salt	1/2 tsp.	2 mL
Cinnamon	1 tsp.	5 mL
Nutmeg	1/4 tsp.	1 mL
Cloves	1/4 tsp.	1 mL
Chopped nuts	1/2 cup	125 mL

Cream butter and both sugars together well. Beat in eggs and vanilla.

Stir remaining ingredients together and add. Mix well. Roll into 2 inch (5 cm) square or round logs. Wrap and chill overnight. Dough may also be frozen. When ready to bake slice thinly. Place on ungreased baking sheet. Bake in 375°F (190°C) oven for about 8 minutes. Makes 4½ to 5 dozen.

Pictured on page 89.

ICE BOX MINCEMEAT COOKIES

These spicy cookies are a bit softer than most ice box varieties.

Butter or margarine, softened	1 cup	250 mL
Brown sugar, packed	1 cup	250 mL
Egg	1	1
Mincemeat	1 cup	250 mL
All–purpose flour	3 cups	750 mL
Baking soda	1 tsp.	5 mL
Salt	1/2 tsp.	2 mL

Cream butter and sugar together. Beat in egg. Add mincemeat.

Stir flour, baking soda and salt together and add. Mix well. Shape into rolls 2 inches (5 cm) in diameter. Wrap and chill overnight. When ready to bake slice thinly and arrange on greased baking sheet. Bake in 400°F (200°C) oven for 6 to 8 minutes. Makes 5 dozen.

Pictured on page 53.

DATE PINWHEELS

Another old favorite. Make one day and bake the next.

FILLING

Dates, chopped	1 lb.	454 g
Granulated sugar	½ cup	125 mL
Water	⅓ cup	75 mL
Finely chopped walnuts	⅔ cup	150 mL

COOKIE DOUGH

Butter or margarine, softened	1 cup	250 mL
Brown sugar, packed	1 cup	250 mL
Granulated sugar	1 cup	250 mL
Eggs	2	2
Vanilla	2 tsp.	10 mL
All–purpose flour	3½ cups	875 mL
Baking soda	1 tsp.	5 mL
Salt	½ tsp.	2 mL

Filling: Simmer dates, sugar and water together until mushy and thickened. Add a bit more water if too dry.

Stir in nuts. Cool.

Cookie Dough: Cream butter with sugars in mixing bowl. Beat in eggs 1 at a time. Add vanilla.

Stir in flour, baking soda and salt. Divide dough into 4 parts. Roll each part ¼ inch (6 mm) thick, in rectangular shape. Spread with date filling. Roll. Chill overnight. Slice ¼ inch (6 mm) thick. Place on greased cookie sheet. Bake in 375°F (190°C) oven for 8 to 10 minutes. Makes about 8 dozen.

Pictured on page 143.

RASPBERRY PINWHEELS: Omit date mixture. Spread dough with a mixture of 1 cup (250 mL) raspberry jam, 1 cup (250 mL) shredded coconut and ½ cup (125 mL) finely chopped nuts. Makes 8 dozen.

CHOCOLATE PINWHEELS: Spread ¼ dough with ½ cup (125 mL) semisweet chocolate chips, melted. Roll, wrap and chill. Bring to room temperature before slicing otherwise chocolate is too hard. These are delicious.

Pictured on page 53.

CHERRY ICE BOX COOKIES

A pretty cookie speckled with bits of red cherries.

Butter (not margarine), softened	1 cup	250 mL
Brown sugar, packed	2/3 cup	150 mL
Eggs	2	2
Almond flavoring	1 tsp.	5 mL
All–purpose flour	2½ cups	625 mL
Candied cherries, cut up	1 cup	250 mL
Finely chopped almonds	½ cup	125 mL

Cream butter and sugar together well. Beat in eggs and almond flavoring.

Add flour, cherries and almonds. Work into dough. Form into rolls 1½ inches (4 cm) or so in diameter. Wrap in waxed paper or plastic. Chill overnight or longer. May also be frozen. To bake, slice thinly and place on greased baking sheet. Bake in 375°F (190°C) oven for 6 to 8 minutes. Makes about 7 dozen.

Pictured on page 89.

SANTA'S WHISKERS

Make these one day and bake the next. One of the most colorful cookies to be found. Reprinted from Company's Coming Holiday Entertaining.

Butter or margarine, softened	1 cup	250 mL
Granulated sugar	1 cup	250 mL
Vanilla	1 tsp.	5 mL
Milk	2 tbsp.	30 mL
All–purpose flour	2½ cups	625 mL
Finely chopped candied cherries, red and green	¾ cup	175 mL
Chopped pecans	½ cup	125 mL
Flaked coconut	1 cup	250 mL

Mix first 7 ingredients together well. Shape into 2 rolls 2 inches (5 cm) in diameter.

Roll in coconut. Cover and chill overnight. Next day slice ¼ inch (1 cm) thick. Arrange on ungreased cookie sheet. Bake in 375°F (190°C) oven for about 10 to 12 minutes or until edges are lightly browned. Makes 4 to 5 dozen.

Pictured on page 17.

SHORTBREAD PINWHEELS

Make one day and bake the next. The rolls of white and chocolate make an interesting design. By omitting cocoa and tinting one half of the dough pink you will have a delicately colored pinwheel.

Butter (not margarine), softened	1 cup	250 mL
Icing (confectioner's) sugar	2/3 cup	150 mL
Vanilla	1/2 tsp.	2 mL
All–purpose flour	2 cups	500 mL
Cocoa	1/4 cup	60 mL

Cream butter and sugar together. Mix in vanilla and flour. Divide dough into 2 equal portions.

To 1 portion add cocoa. Mix well. Roll chocolate portion between 2 layers of waxed paper. Roll to a size of 7½ x 12 inches (19 x 30 cm). Remove top waxed paper. Roll white dough portion between 2 layers of waxed paper. Roll to a size of 7 x 12 inches (18 x 30 cm). Remove top paper. Invert over chocolate layer keeping ends together at 1 end. Chocolate layer will extend a bit at the other end. Remove top paper. Roll from short end with edges even removing bottom paper as you roll. When rolled, complete outside edge will be chocolate. Wrap and chill overnight or longer. When ready to bake slice ⅓ inch (8 mm) thick. Arrange on ungreased baking sheet. Bake in 350°F (180°C) oven for 10 to 12 minutes. Makes about 26 cookies.

Pictured on pages 89, 143 and on cover.

CLOVERLEAF: Omit cocoa. Divide dough into 3 portions, tint 1 yellow, 1 pink, 1 green as shown on page 116. Chill.

CHECKERBOARD: Make 4 ropes, 2 white and 2 chocolate as shown on page 116. Chill.

PINWHEELS

Dark and light stripes in a striking design. Dough may be frozen.

Butter or margarine, softened	1/2 cup	125 mL
Granulated sugar	1/2 cup	125 mL
Egg	1	1
Vanilla	1 tsp.	5 mL
Milk	3 tbsp.	50 mL
All–purpose flour	1¾ cups	375 mL
Baking powder	1/2 tsp.	2 mL
Salt	1/8 tsp.	0.5 mL
Cocoa	2 tbsp.	30 mL
Butter or margarine, softened	1 tbsp.	15 mL

(continued on next page)

Cream first amount of butter and sugar together. Beat in egg, vanilla and milk.

Stir flour, baking powder and salt together and add. Mix into a ball. Divide into 2 equal portions.

To 1 portion add cocoa and remaining butter. Mix well. Roll out each portion between sheets of waxed paper to ⅛ inch (3 mm) thick. Make them the same size in a rectangular shape. Remove top papers. Invert white layer over chocolate. Remove top paper. Roll as for jelly roll, removing bottom paper as you roll. Wrap and chill overnight. To bake slice thinly. Place on ungreased cookie sheet. Bake in 375°F (190°C) oven for about 6 minutes. Makes 4 dozen.

Pictured on page 143.

PEANUT BUTTER ICE BOX COOKIES

Make your cookie dough ahead to have on hand.

Butter or margarine, softened	**½ cup**	**125 mL**
Smooth peanut butter	**½ cup**	**125 mL**
Brown sugar, packed	**1 cup**	**250 mL**
Large eggs	**2**	**2**
Vanilla	**1 tsp.**	**5 mL**
All-purpose flour	**2½ cups**	**625 mL**
Baking powder	**1 tsp.**	**5 mL**
Salt	**1 tsp.**	**5 mL**

In bowl cream butter, peanut butter and sugar. Beat in eggs 1 at a time. Add vanilla.

Reserve ¼ cup (50 mL) flour. Stir rest of flour, baking powder and salt together and mix in. Work in as much reserved flour as you can. Shape into 3 rolls 2 inches (5 cm) in diameter. Wrap and chill overnight or longer. When ready to bake slice thinly. Place on ungreased sheet. Bake in 375°F (190°C) oven for 6 to 8 minutes. Makes 5 dozen.

CHOCOLATE GLAZE

Semi-sweet chocolate squares	**3 x 1 oz.**	**3 x 28 g**
Grated parowax (paraffin)	**2 tbsp.**	**30 mL**

Melt chocolate and parowax together over low heat. Dip corner of cookies. Dry on waxed paper.

Pictured on page 125.

LEMON ICE BOX COOKIES

Crisp and lemony. Add glaze to give an extra touch.

Butter or margarine, softened	1 cup	250 mL
Granulated sugar	¾ cup	175 mL
Eggs	2	2
Grated lemon rind	1 tbsp.	15 mL
All–purpose flour	3 cups	750 mL
Baking powder	½ tsp.	2 mL
Salt	¼ tsp.	1 mL

Cream butter and sugar together well. Beat in eggs, 1 at a time. Add lemon rind.

Stir flour, baking powder and salt together and mix in. Shape into rolls about 2 inches (5 cm) in diameter. Wrap and chill overnight. Dough may also be frozen. Next day slice thinly and place on ungreased cookie sheets. Bake in 375°F (190°C) oven for 7 to 10 minutes. Makes about 5 dozen.

GLAZE: Mix ½ cup (125 mL) icing (confectioner's) sugar with enough lemon juice to make a barely pourable glaze. Add yellow food coloring if desired. Spread on cookies.

Pictured on page 125.

ICE BOX GINGER COOKIES

These crisp cookies keep well. A popular flavor.

Butter or margarine, softened	1 cup	250 mL
Granulated sugar	1½ cups	375 mL
Egg	1	1
Corn syrup	2 tbsp.	30 mL
Baking soda	2 tsp.	10 mL
Warm water	1 tbsp.	15 mL
Grated rind of large whole orange	1	1
All–purpose flour	3 cups	750 mL
Ginger	2 tsp.	10 mL
Cinnamon	2 tsp.	10 mL
Cloves	½ tsp.	2 mL

(continued on next page)

Cream butter and sugar together. Beat in egg and corn syrup.

Dissolve baking soda in water and mix in.

Stir in remaining ingredients. Mix well. Shape into 2 inch (5 cm) rolls. Wrap and chill overnight or longer. Dough may be frozen. When ready to bake, slice thinly. Place on ungreased baking sheet. Bake in 400°F (200°C) oven for 8 to 10 minutes. Makes 6 dozen, 3 inch (7.5 cm) cookies.

Pictured on page 53.

BUTTERSCOTCH COOKIES

A favorite flavor for everybody. Crisp.

Butter or margarine, softened	1 cup	250 mL
Brown sugar, packed	2 cups	500 mL
Eggs	2	2
Vanilla	1 tsp	5 mL
Chopped walnuts	1 cup	250 mL
All-purpose flour	3 cups	750 mL
Baking soda	1 tsp.	5 mL

Cream butter and sugar together in mixing bowl. Beat in eggs 1 at a time. Stir in vanilla and nuts.

Stir flour and baking soda together and add to mixture. Shape into rolls about 2 inches (5 mL) in diameter. Wrap in waxed paper or plastic and chill overnight or longer. When ready to bake, slice however many you want and freeze the rest of the dough. To bake, slice thinly and arrange on ungreased cookie sheet. Bake in 350°F (180°C) oven for about 8 to 10 minutes. Makes about 12 dozen.

Pictured on page 71.

Paré Pointer

The best thing for nail biting is sharp teeth.

ICE BOX RIBBONS

Three pretty layers baked as one cookie. Freezes well before or after baking.

Butter or margarine, softened	1 cup	250 mL
Granulated sugar	1 cup	250 mL
Egg	1	1
Vanilla	1 tsp.	5 mL
All–purpose flour	2½ cups	675 mL
Baking powder	1 tsp.	5 mL
Salt	¼ tsp.	1 mL
Red food coloring		
Chopped candied red cherries	¼ cup	60 mL
Semisweet chocolate chips, melted	⅓ cup	75 mL
Chopped nuts	⅓ cup	75 mL
Coconut	⅓ cup	75 mL

Cream butter and sugar together. Beat in egg and vanilla.

Stir flour, baking powder and salt together and mix in. Divide dough into 3 equal parts.

First Layer: To 1 part of dough mix in enough red food coloring to tint a pretty pink. Add cherries. Combine and pack into 8 x 4 inch (20 x 10 cm) foil–lined loaf pan.

Second Layer: To second part of dough mix in chocolate and nuts. Pack evenly over first layer.

Third Layer: To last part of dough mix in coconut. Pack over second layer. Wrap and chill overnight. When ready to bake remove foil from dough. Cut into slices ¼ inch (6 mm) thick. Then cut each slice into 3 pieces. Arrange on ungreased cookie sheet. Bake in 350°F (180°C) oven for 10 to 12 minutes. Makes about 5½ dozen.

Pictured on page 17.

Paré Pointer

With an earthquake and a forest fire you have shake and bake.

PEANUT BUTTER CUPS

A real treat for any age. Takes extra time to dip in chocolate.

Smooth peanut butter	1½ cups	375 mL
Butter or margarine, softened	¼ cup	60 mL
Icing (confectioner's) sugar	2 cups	500 mL
Vanilla	1 tsp.	5 mL
Semisweet chocolate chips	2 cups	500 mL
Grated parowax (paraffin)	⅓ cup	75 mL

Mix first 4 ingredients together. Shape into 1 inch (2.5 cm) balls. May be shaped into logs as well using same amount of dough.

Melt chocolate chips and wax in small heavy saucepan over low heat. Dip balls, drain and place on waxed paper. Makes about 7½ dozen.

Pictured on page 17.

CREAMY SNOWBALLS

If you have a sweet tooth these are for you. Creamy.

Cream cheese, softened	4 oz.	125 g
Icing (confectioner's) sugar	2 cups	500 mL
Milk	2 tbsp.	30 mL
Semisweet chocolate chips, melted	⅔ cup	150 mL
Vanilla	½ tsp.	2 mL
Miniature colored marshmallows	3 cups	750 mL

Coconut

Combine first 5 ingredients together in bowl. Beat together until smooth.

Fold in marshmallows. Mix well. Chill for 30 minutes.

Shape into 1½ inch (3 cm) balls.

Roll in coconut. These freeze well. Makes about 3½ dozen.

Pictured on page 17.

DATE COCONUT BALLS

With these in the freezer you will always have a party–type cookie on hand. Made in a saucepan.

Chopped dates	1½ cups	350 mL
Brown sugar, packed	1 cup	250 mL
Butter or margarine	1 tbsp.	15 mL
Eggs	2	2
Vanilla	1 tsp.	5 mL
Crisp rice cereal	2 cups	450 mL
Finely chopped nuts	½ cup	125 mL
Finely chopped cherries	¼ cup	60 mL

Shredded coconut

Combine dates, sugar, butter, eggs and vanilla in saucepan. Heat. Cook, stirring constantly for about 5 minutes.

Stir in cereal, nuts and cherries. Cool until mixture is warm. Shape into 1 inch (2.5 cm) balls.

Roll balls in coconut. Butter hands to prevent dough from sticking. Makes 4 dozen.

Pictured on page 143.

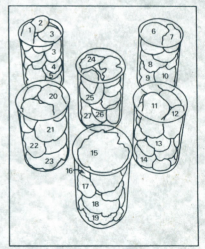

COCONUT LOGS

Like your favorite coconut chocolate bar. No baking.

Icing (confectioner's) sugar	2 cups	450 mL
Flaked coconut	2 cups	450 mL
Milk	2 tbsp.	30 mL
Butter or margarine, softened	1 tbsp.	15 mL
Semisweet chocolate chips	1 cup	250 mL
Grated parowax (paraffin)	3 tbsp.	50 mL

Mix first 4 ingredients together well. Shape into thumb size logs.

Melt chocolate chips and parowax in small saucepan over low heat. Dip logs in chocolate to cover. Drain and place on waxed paper. Makes 2½ dozen.

Pictured on page 17.

GINGER CHOCO COOKIES

These no–bake cookies are made from ginger snap crumbs. They are soft and creamy.

Semisweet chocolate chips	2 cups	500 mL
Sour cream	½ cup	125 mL
Lemon juice	1 tsp.	5 mL
Ginger snap crumbs	2 cups	500 mL
Icing (confectioner's) sugar	1 cup	250 mL

Melt chocolate chips in sour cream and lemon juice in medium size, heavy saucepan over low heat. Stir often to hasten melting. Be careful not to boil. Remove from heat.

Add cookie crumbs and icing sugar. Stir to moisten. Shape into 1 inch (2.5 cm) balls. These may be left as is or rolled in icing sugar or dipped in chocolate glaze. Makes about 6 dozen.

CHOCOLATE GLAZE: Mix 1 cup (250 mL) icing (confectioner's) sugar with 2 tbsp. (30 mL) cocoa. Add enough water to make a barely pourable glaze. Dip tops of cookie balls and leave to dry on tray.

Pictured on page 107.

CHOCOLATE CRISPS

No oven to make these chocolaty good drops.

Semisweet chocolate chips	2 cups	500 mL
Crisp rice cereal	2 cups	500 mL
Shredded coconut	1 cup	250 mL

Melt chips in heavy saucepan over low heat.

Mix in cereal and coconut. Drop by spoonfuls onto waxed paper. Let harden. Makes 3 dozen.

Pictured on page 125.

BOILED CHOCOLATE COOKIES

This is probably the most used recipe of young first–time cooks. No oven required.

Butter or margarine	½ cup	125 mL
Milk	½ cup	125 mL
Granulated sugar	2 cups	500 mL
Cocoa	½ cup	125 mL
Rolled oats	2½ cups	625 mL

Put butter, milk, sugar and cocoa into saucepan. Bring to a boil stirring often. Boil 5 minutes.

Remove from heat. Stir in rolled oats. Drop by teaspoonfuls onto waxed paper. Makes about 4 dozen.

Variation: To make these more special, coconut, cherries and/or nuts may be added.

Pictured on page 89.

Paré Pointer

A rug you take up and shake and medicine you shake up and take.

PEANUT BUTTER DROPS

A splendid variation of a boiled chocolate cookie.

Butter or margarine	½ cup	125 mL
Milk	½ cup	125 mL
Granulated sugar	1¾ cups	425 mL
Cocoa	½ cup	125 mL
Rolled oats	3 cups	750 mL
Smooth peanut butter	½ cup	125 mL

Measure first 4 ingredients into medium saucepan. Bring to a boil over medium heat stirring often. Boil for 3 minutes. Remove from heat.

Add rolled oats and peanut butter. Mix well. Drop by spoonfuls onto waxed paper. Freezes. Makes about 5 dozen.

Pictured on page 107.

CRACKER SNACK

From crackers come these peanut butter cookies. Dipped in choco-late, they become an extra special treat. No baking.

Round mild flavored crackers	48	48
Smooth peanut butter	1 cup	250 mL
Semisweet chocolate squares	8 x 1 oz.	8 x 28 g
Grated parowax (paraffin)	¼ cup	50 mL

Spread crackers liberally with peanut butter, making sandwich style. It is not necessary to use the amount given.

Melt chocolate with wax over hot water. Dip sandwiched crackers, then place on waxed paper. Makes 2 dozen.

PRETZEL SNACK: Dip pretzels in chocolate–wax mixture. A quick treat.

Pictured on page 107.

CREAM CHEESE BALLS

These creamy cookies need no baking. The addition of cherries gives them color.

Cream cheese, softened	8 oz.	250 mL
Icing (confectioner's) sugar	1 cup	250 mL
Coconut	2/3 cup	150 mL
Maraschino cherries, finely chopped	15	15
Crushed pineapple, drained	14 oz.	398 mL
Vanilla wafer crumbs	2 cups	450 mL
COATING		
Butter or margarine	2 tbsp.	30 mL
Granulated sugar	1 tbsp.	15 mL
Graham cracker crumbs	3/4 cup	175 mL

Beat cream cheese and icing sugar together. Mix in coconut and cherries. Stir in pineapple and crumbs. Chill for 30 minutes. Shape into 1 inch (2.5 cm) balls.

Coating: Melt butter in small saucepan. Remove from heat. Stir in sugar and crumbs. Roll cookies in this mixture. Freezes well. Makes about 5 dozen.

Pictured on page 53.

NOODLE POWER

These little stacks are shiny and ever so good. They are softer and easier to bite into than other similar cookies.

Semisweet chocolate chips	1 cup	250 mL
Butterscotch chips	1 cup	250 mL
Butter or margarine	1/4 cup	50 mL
Smooth peanut butter	1/4 cup	50 mL
Peanuts	1 cup	250 mL
Dry Chinese noodles	2 cups	500 mL

Melt first 4 ingredients in large saucepan over low heat. Stir often. Remove from heat.

Mix in peanuts and noodles. Spoon into mounds on waxed paper. Mixture will seem soft but it will firm upon standing. May be chilled to hasten hardening. Makes 2½ dozen.

Pictured on page 125.

COCONUT PEAKS

Chocolate peaks take the spotlight when these are served. A no–bake treat.

Butter or margarine	¼ cup	60 mL
Icing (confectioner's) sugar	2 cups	450 mL
Light cream	2 tbsp.	30 mL
Flaked coconut	3 cups	675 mL
Semisweet chocolate chips	1 cup	250 mL
Butter or margarine	1 tbsp.	15 mL

Melt first amount of butter in saucepan. Remove from heat. Stir in icing sugar, cream and coconut. Shape into small balls, then squeeze top to form peaks which resemble tiny haystacks. Place on tray. Put in refrigerator, uncovered. Let dry overnight.

In small saucepan, over low heat, melt chocolate chips and remaining butter together. Stir often. Dip tops of peaks. Freezes well. Makes 2½ dozen.

Pictured on page 17.

PEANUT BUTTER BALLS

These crispy–crunch balls are the best! Fabulous. My favorite.

Smooth peanut butter	1 cup	250 mL
Icing (confectioner's) sugar	1 cup	250 mL
Crisp rice cereal	1 cup	250 mL
Finely chopped walnuts	½ cup	125 mL
Butter or margarine, softened	1 tbsp.	15 mL
Semisweet chocolate squares	4 x 1 oz.	4 x 28 g
Grated parowax (paraffin)	2 tbsp.	30 mL

Measure first 5 ingredients into bowl. With your hands, mix together well. Shape into 1 inch (2.5 cm) balls. Chill for 2 to 3 hours.

Melt chocolate chips and wax together. Dip balls to coat, drain and place on waxed paper. Makes 4½ to 5 dozen.

Pictured on page 125.

GLAZED COFFEE BALLS

Not even a saucepan is needed for these little morsels. Just mix, shape, then dip in coffee flavored glaze.

Graham cracker crumbs	2 cups	450 mL
Icing (confectioner's) sugar	½ cup	125 mL
Finely chopped pecans	½ cup	125 mL
Hot water	½ cup	125 mL
Instant coffee granules	1 tsp.	5 mL
Butter or margarine	2 tbsp.	30 mL
GLAZE		
Icing (confectioner's) sugar	1 cup	250 mL
Butter or margarine, softened	1 tbsp.	15 mL
Prepared coffee	1 tbsp.	15 mL

Measure crumbs, icing sugar and pecans into bowl.

In measuring cup measure hot water. Stir in coffee granules and butter to melt. Pour over crumb mixture. Stir well. Form into small balls. Dip in glaze.

Glaze: Mix sugar, butter and coffee, adding more sugar or coffee if needed for proper consistency. Dip balls in glaze. Let dry on waxed paper. Makes about 40.

Pictured on page 125.

COCONUT FRUIT BITES

These tangy little balls have no sugar added. No baking. Just mix and shape.

Dates, cut up	1 cup	250 mL
Dried apricots, cut up	1 cup	250 mL
Raisins	1 cup	250 mL
Chopped walnuts	1 cup	250 mL
Coconut	1 cup	250 mL
Coconut		

Grind dates, apricots and raisins or use food processor.

Add nuts and first amount of coconut. Shape into 1 inch (2.5 cm) balls. Roll in coconut. Freezes well. Makes about 4 dozen.

Pictured on page 89.

CHOCO COCONUT BALLS

These dark colored balls have white centers. No oven needed.

Butter or margarine	1/4 cup	60 mL
Sweetened condensed milk	2/3 cup	150 mL
Icing (confectioner's) sugar	3 1/3 cups	750 mL
Coconut	1/2 cup	125 mL
Chopped pecans or walnuts	1 cup	250 mL
Semisweet chocolate chips	1 cup	250 mL
Grated parowax (paraffin)	3 tbsp.	50 mL

Melt butter in saucepan. Stir in milk and sugar. Remove from heat.

Add coconut and nuts. Add more icing sugar if it seems too soft. Chill. Roll into 1 inch (2.5 cm) balls.

Melt chocolate chips and wax in small saucepan over low heat. Dip balls to coat. Drain and place on waxed paper. Makes about 6 dozen.

Pictured on page 125.

COCONUT BALLS

These are not too sweet. No baking.

Sweetened condensed milk	11 oz.	300 mL
Semisweet chocolate chips	2/3 cup	150 mL
Chopped nuts	1/2 cup	125 mL
Graham cracker crumbs	2 1/2 cups	575 mL
Coconut		

In bowl mix first 4 ingredients together. Shape into 1 inch (2.5 cm) balls.

Roll in coconut. Makes 5 dozen.

Pictured on page 89.

PEANUT BUTTER CHIP BALLS

Just a few ingredients for these. Dipping is optional.

Smooth peanut butter	1 cup	250 mL
Sweetened condensed milk	½ cup	125 mL
Icing (confectioner's) sugar	½ cup	125 mL
Semisweet chocolate chips	1 cup	250 mL

Mix all ingredients together. Shape into balls. Place on waxed paper. Chill to set. Makes about 4 dozen.

CHOCOLATE COATING: Melt 1 cup (250 mL) semisweet chocolate chips and 3 tbsp. (50 mL) grated parowax (paraffin) in heavy saucepan or over hot water in double boiler. Dip balls and place on waxed paper to dry.

Pictured on page 125.

TOFFEE COOKIES

These are ever so yummy. No baking required.

Caramels (about 36)	8 oz.	225 g
Cream (light)	3 tbsp.	50 mL
Cornflakes	2 cups	450 mL
Crisp rice cereal	1 cup	225 mL
Coconut	½ cup	125 mL

Put caramels and cream into large heavy saucepan over low heat to melt.

Add remaining ingredients. Stir to coat. Drop by spoonfuls onto greased surface. Leave to harden. Makes about 3½ dozen.

Pictured on page 35.

Pare Pointer

All sick ponies go to the horse-pital.

PEANUT BUTTER BITES

A snap to make. No baking for this grand cookie. Dip tops in melted chocolate chips and nuts for a festive look.

Smooth peanut butter	½ cup	125 mL
Icing (confectioner's) sugar	½ cup	125 mL
Graham cracker crumbs	½ cup	125 mL
Finely chopped nuts, cocoa, icing sugar, chocolate sprinkles		

Mix first 3 ingredients together. Shape into 1 inch (2.5 cm) balls.

Roll in nuts, cocoa, icing sugar or chocolate sprinkles. Freezes well. Makes about 3 dozen.

Pictured on page 89.

APRICOT JAM BALLS

Make these no–bake cookies in a jiffy.

Apricot jam	½ cup	125 mL
Butter or margarine	2 tbsp.	30 mL
Graham cracker crumbs	2 cups	500 mL
Rum flavoring	½ tsp.	2 mL
Medium coconut		

Combine jam and butter in medium size saucepan. Heat and stir to boiling. Remove from heat.

Stir in graham crumbs and flavoring. Roll into 1 inch (2.5 cm) balls.

Roll in medium coconut. Makes 28.

Pictured on page 107.

Pare Pointer

Cinderella couldn't play football. Her coach was a pumpkin.

BUTTERSCOTCH NOODLES

Make these in a saucepan. Quick and easy.

Butterscotch chips	2 cups	500 mL
Butter or margarine	½ cup	125 mL
Peanuts	1 cup	250 mL
Dry Chinese chow mein noodles	2 cups	500 mL

Melt chips and butter in heavy saucepan over low heat. Stir to hasten melting. Stir in peanuts and noodles. Drop by spoonfuls onto waxed paper. Makes 3 dozen.

PEANUT BUTTER NOODLES: Add 2 tbsp. (30 mL) smooth peanut butter.

Pictured on page 107.

PEANUT GRAHAM MORSELS

No need to bake these flavorful bites.

Butter or margarine, softened	½ cup	125 mL
Smooth peanut butter	¾ cup	175 mL
Coconut or chopped nuts	½ cup	125 mL
Icing (confectioner's) sugar	1¾ cups	425 mL
Graham cracker crumbs	1 cup	250 mL
Semisweet chocolate chips	1 cup	250 mL
Grated parowax (paraffin)	3 tbsp.	50 mL

Mix first 5 ingredients together in bowl. Shape into 1 inch (2.5 cm) balls and logs using same amount of dough for logs.

Melt chocolate chips with parowax. Either dip to coat or just dip tops. Place on waxed paper. Makes 6 dozen.

Pictured on page 125.

Pare Pointer

Definition of a snake: a tail without a body.

CREAMY MORSELS

These good rich rolls begin in a saucepan followed by chilling. Roll into logs and then in coconut.

Semisweet chocolate chips	1 cup	250 mL
Butterscotch chips	1 cup	250 mL
Cream cheese, softened	8 oz.	250 g
Candied cherries, quartered	1 cup	250 mL
Tiny marshmallows, halved	2½ cups	625 mL
Coconut		

Put chocolate and butterscotch chips in medium size saucepan over low heat. Melt, stirring often. Remove from heat.

Add cheese in small pieces. Stir in cherries and marshmallows. Chill until it starts to firm.

Shape into thumb size logs. Roll in coconut. Freezes. Makes about 5 dozen.

Pictured on page 107.

PEANUT BALLS

Chewy and much like toffee. Good peanut flavor. No baking needed.

Finely chopped peanuts	3 cups	675 mL
Sweetened condensed milk	11 oz.	300 mL
Ground peanuts to coat		

Combine peanuts and milk in heavy saucepan. Heat and stir until boiling. Stir constantly for 5 minutes until mixture forms a ball and leaves sides of pan. Cool to room temperature. Shape into 1 inch (2.5 cm) balls.

Roll in ground peanuts. Makes about 4½ dozen.

Pictured on page 89.

Paré Pointer

Billy eats with his knife because his fork leaks.

APRICOT BALLS

No cooking for this one. Not too sweet.

Ground dried apricots	½ lb.	225 g
Medium coconut	2 cups	450 mL
Icing (confectioner's) sugar	¼ cup	60 mL
Finely chopped nuts	½ cup	125 mL
Sweetened condensed milk	½ cup	125 mL
Grated orange rind	½ tsp.	2 mL

Mix all ingredients together. Roll into 1 inch (2.5 cm) balls. Chill. Makes 5 dozen.

Pictured on page 53.

CHOCOLATE PEANUT DROPS

Peanut butter adds to the flavor of these saucepan cookies.

Milk	½ cup	125 mL
Butter or margarine	½ cup	125 mL
Granulated sugar	2 cups	500 mL
Cocoa	6 tbsp.	100 mL
Smooth peanut butter	¾ cup	175 mL
Vanilla	1 tsp.	5 mL
Rolled oats	3 cups	750 mL
Chopped nuts (optional)	½ cup	125 mL

Put milk, butter, sugar and cocoa in medium size saucepan. Heat and stir until boiling. Remove from heat.

Stir in peanut butter and vanilla. Add rolled oats and nuts. Mix. Drop by spoonfuls onto waxed paper. Makes about 4½ dozen.

Pictured on page 71.

Paré Pointer

All he talks about is his ancestors. His family is better dead than alive.

GRANOLA STACKS

A tasty mixture of cereal and raisins combined with melted chips. No oven needed.

Semisweet chocolate chips	1 cup	250 mL
Butterscotch chips	1 cup	250 mL
Granola cereal	1¼ cups	300 mL
Raisins (optional)	¼ cup	50 mL

In medium saucepan melt chocolate and butterscotch chips over low heat. Remove from heat. Stir in cereal and raisins. Drop by spoonfuls onto waxed paper. Makes about 2½ dozen.

Pictured on page 53.

SAUCEPAN COCONUT BALLS

Sunflower seeds add a special nutty flavor.

Eggs	2	2
Granulated sugar	1 cup	250 mL
Raisins	1 cup	250 mL
Chopped nuts	1 cup	250 mL
Coconut	1 cup	250 mL
Sunflower seeds	¼ cup	60 mL
Vanilla	1 tsp.	5 mL
Almond flavoring	⅛ tsp.	0.5 mL
Icing (confectioner's) sugar		

Beat eggs in medium saucepan. Beat in sugar. Add raisins and nuts. Cook and stir over medium heat until eggs thicken. Remove from heat.

Stir in coconut, sunflower seeds, vanilla and almond flavoring. Cool.

Shape into balls. Roll in icing sugar. Freezes. Makes about 3½ dozen.

Pictured on page 89.

ORANGE BALLS

These unbaked cookies have a real orange flavor.

Vanilla wafer crumbs	4 cups	900 mL
Butter or margarine, softened	½ cup	125 mL
Icing (confectioner's) sugar	2½ cups	575 mL
Chopped pecans or walnuts	½ cup	125 mL
Frozen concentrated orange juice, thawed	6 oz.	170 g
Medium coconut or chocolate sprinkles	2 cups	450 mL

Combine first 5 ingredients in bowl. Mix well. Shape into 1 inch (2.5 cm) balls.

Roll in coconut. Freezes well. Makes 5 dozen.

Pictured on page 89.

BUTTER BALLS

Crisp and mellow with a peanut butter flavor. No–bake.

Butterscotch chips	1 cup	250 mL
Smooth peanut butter	½ cup	125 mL
Crisp rice cereal	3 cups	750 mL

Melt chips and peanut butter in saucepan. Stir often. Remove from heat. Mix in rice cereal. Drop by spoonfuls onto waxed paper. Makes about 3 dozen.

Pictured on page 89.

Paré Pointer

"Your money or your life." "Take my life. I need my money to live on."

These are crisp thin wafers put together with a creamy chocolate filling.

Butter or margarine, softened	½ cup	125 mL
Granulated sugar	¼ cup	60 mL
Semisweet chocolate square, melted	1 oz.	28 g
All–purpose flour	1 cup	250 mL

In mixing bowl cream together butter, sugar and chocolate.

Mix in flour. Cover and chill overnight. Roll out on lightly floured surface. Cut into squares 2 x 2 inches (5 x 5 cm). Bake on greased cookie sheet in 350°F (180°C) oven for about 10 to 12 minutes. When cool, put together with icing and finish as recipe states. Makes about 28 cookie sandwiches.

ICING

Butter or margarine, softened	2 tbsp.	30 mL
Icing (confectioner's) sugar	⅓ cup	75 mL
Semisweet chocolate chips, melted	⅓ cup	75 mL
Semisweet chocolate squares, melted	14 x 1 oz.	14 x 28 g

With a spoon, beat first 3 ingredients together. Spread between cookies to make sandwich style.

Place a few cookies on rack over plate. Spoon semisweet chocolate over, covering tops and sides. Place on waxed paper to set. Return drained chocolate on plate back to saucepan as it collects.

Pictured on page 107.

Paré Pointer

The most noble dog of all is a hot dog. It feeds the hand that bites it.

OATCAKES

Tender and not sweet. Traditional oatcakes used to contain lard or drippings. Today butter or margarine may be used.

All–purpose flour	1½ cups	375 mL
Granulated sugar	½ cup	125 mL
Baking powder	1 tsp.	5 mL
Salt	½ tsp.	2 mL
Lard	¾ cup	175 mL
Rolled oats	1½ cups	375 mL
Water	6 tbsp.	100 mL

Stir flour, sugar, baking powder and salt together in bowl. Cut in lard until crumbly.

Mix in rolled oats. Sprinkle with water. Work into a ball with your hands. Roll out fairly thin. Cut into 2½ inch (6 cm) circles. Arrange on lightly greased cookie sheet. Bake in 350°F (180°C) oven for about 15 minutes. Makes 2½ dozen.

Pictured on page 125.

Firm and lemony.

Butter or margarine, softened	½ cup	125 mL
Granulated sugar	½ cup	125 mL
Egg	1	1
Sweetened condensed milk	⅔ cup	150 mL
Lemon juice	2 tbsp.	30 mL
Grated lemon rind	1 tbsp.	15 mL
Vanilla	1 tsp.	5 mL
All–purpose flour	2¼ cups	550 mL
Baking powder	2 tsp.	10 mL
Salt	½ tsp.	2 mL

Cut butter and sugar together well. Beat in egg. Add milk, lemon juice, lemon rind and vanilla.

Stir flour, baking powder and salt together and add. Mix well. Roll out on lightly floured surface. Cut into any desired shapes from circles to Christmas trees. Bake in 350°F (180°C) oven for about 8 minutes. Glaze. Makes approximately 6 dozen, 2 inch (5 cm) cookies.

GLAZE

Icing (confectioner's) sugar	¾ cup	175 mL
Lemon juice	1½ tsp.	7 mL
Water	2 tsp.	10 mL

Mix all 3 ingredients together adding more sugar or water if needed to make a barely pourable glaze. Frost cookies.

Pictured on page 107.

Paré Pointer

You get stucco when you sit on gummo.

COFFEE FINGERS

These short-textured little rolls are covered with nuts.

Butter or margarine, softened	1 cup	250 mL
Brown sugar, packed	1/2 cup	125 mL
Icing (confectioner's) sugar	1/4 cup	60 mL
Instant coffee granules, crushed	1 tsp.	5 mL
Egg yolk	1	1
All-purpose flour	2 cups	500 mL
Egg white, fork beaten	1	1
Finely chopped nuts	1 1/2 cups	375 mL

Measure first 5 ingredients into mixing bowl. Stir.

Add flour. Mix well. Roll 1/2 inch (1.5 cm) thick on lightly floured surface. Cut into fingers 1/2 x 2 inches (1.5 x 5 cm).

Dip into egg white, roll in nuts and place on greased cookie sheet. Bake in 300°F (150°C) oven for 20 to 25 minutes. Makes 4 dozen.

Pictured on page 107.

ROLLED GINGER COOKIES

A super dough that bakes sturdy men, lollipops and hanging orna-ments. The glaze stays sticky for about thirty minutes to allow for lots of decorating trials and errors. May also be iced and decorated.

Butter or margarine, softened	1/4 cup	60 mL
Granulated sugar	1/2 cup	125 mL
Molasses	1/2 cup	125 mL
Water	1/3 cup	75 mL
All-purpose flour	3 1/4 cups	750 mL
Baking soda	1 tsp.	5 mL
Ginger	1 tsp.	5 mL
Cinnamon	1/2 tsp.	2 mL
Cloves	1/4 tsp.	1 mL
Salt	1/2 tsp.	2 mL
Glaze and decorations		

(continued on next page)

In mixing bowl cream butter and sugar together. Add molasses and water.

Mix in remaining ingredients. Roll out on lightly floured board. Cut dough into shapes of gingerbread men and circles. Make hole ½ inch (1.25 cm) from top edge using milkshake straw. To make lollipops, shape ⅓ cup (75 mL) dough into ball. Insert small wooden stick. Arrange on greased cookie sheet. Press with glass to ¼ inch (6 mm) thick. Bake in 350°F (180°C) oven for 8 to 10 minutes. Cook thicker cookies a bit longer. Makes about 2 dozen men and circles.

Glazing and Decorating: Brush tops of cookies with warm corn syrup. Apply decorations to your liking.

Pictured on pages 17 and 35.

GRAHAM CRACKERS

Crisp and flavorful similar to commercial varieties.

Butter or margarine, softened	½ cup	125 mL
Brown sugar, packed	½ cup	125 mL
Honey or corn syrup	¼ cup	60 mL
Vanilla	1 tsp.	5 mL
Water	½ cup	125 mL
Graham or wholewheat flour	2 cups	500 mL
All–purpose flour	1 cup	250 mL
Baking powder	1 tsp.	5 mL
Baking soda	½ tsp.	2 mL
Salt	½ tsp.	2 mL
Cinnamon	¼ tsp.	1 mL

Measure butter, brown sugar and honey into bowl. Cream well. Add vanilla and water.

Stir remaining ingredients together and add. Mix well. Roll paper thin on lightly floured surface. Cut into 2½ inch (6.5 cm) squares and place on ungreased baking sheet. Use ruler for even cutting. Prick evenly with fork. Bake in 375°F (190°C) oven for about 8 to 10 minutes. Makes 7 dozen.

Pictured on page 125.

DATE FILLED OATMEAL COOKIES

This makes a huge batch. They soften after being filled with date filling. Make small for tea and larger for regular use.

Butter or margarine, softened	2 cups	500 mL
Brown sugar, packed	2 cups	500 mL
Milk	1 cup	250 mL
All–purpose flour	4 cups	1 L
Rolled oats	4 cups	1 L
Baking powder	5 tsp.	25 mL
Salt	1 tsp.	5 mL

Cream butter and sugar together well. Slowly mix in milk.

Add remaining ingredients. Mix well. Roll out thinly on lightly floured board. Cut into 2½ inch (6.5 cm) rounds. Place on ungreased baking sheets. Bake in 350°F (180°C) oven for 8 to 10 minutes. Cool. Fill with Date Filling, below, to form sandwich cookies. Makes 15 dozen singles, 7½ dozen date–filled.

DATE FILLING

Chopped dates	½ lb.	250 g
Granulated sugar	⅓ cup	75 mL
Water	⅔ cup	150 mL

Combine dates, sugar and water in saucepan. Bring to boil. Simmer, stirring often, until mushy. Add more water if too dry. If too runny simmer longer to evaporate moisture. Cool and spread between cookies.

Pictured on page 125.

Paré Pointer

She thinks doctors should keep practising medicine until they get it right.

The best jam sandwich going.

Butter or margarine, softened	1 cup	250 mL
Brown sugar, packed	¼ cup	60 mL
Granulated sugar	¼ cup	60 mL
Corn syrup	½ cup	125 mL
Eggs	2	2
Vanilla	1 tsp.	5 mL
All–purpose flour	3 cups	750 mL
Baking powder	½ tsp.	2 mL
Salt	½ tsp.	2 mL

Strawberry, raspberry or black currant
   jam or jelly

Cream butter and both sugars well. Beat in corn syrup, eggs and vanilla.

Mix in flour, baking powder and salt. Roll ⅛ inch (3 mm) thick on lightly floured surface. Cut in 2¾ inch (7 cm) circles. Arrange on greased cookie sheet.

Spread ½ tsp. (2 mL) jam on bottom circle leaving ⅜ inch (1 cm) around the outside edge bare. Cut small hole in top circle and place over jam. Press outside edge lightly with fingers. Bake in 350°F (180°C) oven for 8 to 10 minutes. These may be baked separately if you prefer and sandwiched together with jam later. Makes about 20.

Pictured on page 53.

Paré Pointer

He shoots his mouth off so often that he must brush his teeth with gun powder.

ARROWROOT BISCUITS

The addition of arrowroot flour makes this type of cookie easier to digest than others.

Butter or margarine, softened	1/4 cup	60 mL
Granulated sugar	1/2 cup	125 mL
Egg	1	1
Vanilla	1/2 tsp.	2 mL
All–purpose flour	1 cup	225 mL
Arrowroot flour	1/2 cup	125 mL
Baking powder	1/2 tsp.	2 mL
Salt	1/4 tsp.	1 mL

Cream butter and sugar together. Beat in egg and vanilla.

Stir remaining ingredients together and add. Mix well. Roll 1/8 inch (3 mm) thick on floured surface. Cut into 2 1/2 inch (6.5 cm) rounds. Place on greased baking sheet. Prick with fork. Bake in 350°F (180°C) oven until golden, about 8 to 10 minutes. Allow a bit more time if rolled thicker. These do not spread. Makes 3 1/2 dozen.

Pictured on page 53.

PEANUT WAFERS

A hard thin cookie. Once you nibble on one you will find them addictive.

Eggs	2	2
Ground peanuts	2 cups	500 mL
Granulated sugar	1 cup	250 mL
Butter or margarine, softened	2 tbsp.	30 mL
Milk	2 tbsp.	30 mL
Salt	1 tsp.	5 mL
All–purpose flour	2 cups	500 mL

Mix all ingredients together. Roll paper thin on lightly floured surface. Cut into 2 inch (5 cm) squares. Place on ungreased baking sheet. Bake in 375°F (190°C) oven for 9 to 10 minutes. Watch carefully. They burn easily. Makes about 5 dozen.

Pictured on page 107.

These chocolate sandwich cookies are wonderful with tea or coffee.
Bourbon in the filling may be exchanged for rum or brandy flavoring.

Butter or margarine, softened	6 tbsp.	100 mL
Granulated sugar	¼ cup	60 mL
Cocoa	¼ cup	60 mL
All–purpose flour	1½ cups	375 mL
Corn syrup	2 tbsp.	30 mL
Egg	1	1
Granulated sugar for garnish		

Combine butter, sugar, cocoa and flour in bowl. Mix until crumbly.

Add syrup and egg. Blend together. If necessary, add a bit more flour to make a firm dough. Knead lightly. Roll out thinly. Cut into rectangles 1 x 3 inches (2.5 x 7.5 cm). Place on greased cookie sheet. Bake in 350°F (180°C) oven for 10 to 15 minutes until they darken in color.

Sprinkle with sugar as soon as removed from oven. Sandwich together with filling. Makes 2½ dozen.

FILLING

Butter or margarine, softened	½ cup	125 mL
Icing (confectioner's) sugar	1 cup	250 mL
Semisweet chocolate chips, melted and cooled	⅓ cup	75 mL
Bourbon (optional)	1 tsp.	5 mL

Mix all together. Spread between cookies.

Pictured on page 143.

Paré Pointer

If you cross poison ivy with a four–leaf clover, would you get a rash of good luck?

CINNAMON ROLLS

A delicious cookie that isn't too sweet.

Butter or margarine, softened	1 cup	250 mL
Cream cheese, softened	4 oz.	125 g
Granulated sugar	¾ cup	175 mL
Egg	1	1
Vanilla	1 tsp.	5 mL
All–purpose flour	2¼ cups	550 mL
Baking soda	½ tsp.	2 mL
Salt	¼ tsp.	1 mL
Melted butter	1 tbsp.	15 mL
Cinnamon sprinkle		
Brown sugar sprinkle		

Cream butter, cream cheese and sugar together well. Beat in egg and vanilla.

Stir flour, baking soda and salt together and add. Mix well. Roll dough ¼ inch (6 mm) thick into rectangle about 9 x 13 inches (22 x 33 cm).

Brush with melted butter. Spinkle with cinnamon and brown sugar. Beginning at long side, roll up like a jelly roll. Chill ½ hour. Slice ½ inch (1.25 cm) thick. Arrange on greased baking sheet. Bake in 350°F (180°C) oven for 10 to 12 minutes. Makes about 4½ dozen.

Pictured on page 53.

SOUR CREAM NUT ROLLS

Little envelopes filled with nutty almond filling.

All–purpose flour	2 cups	500 mL
Butter or margarine, softened	1 cup	250 mL
Sour cream	½ cup	125 mL
Egg yolks	2	2
FILLING		
Ground almonds	2½ cups	625 mL
Granulated sugar	½ cup	125 mL
Milk	¼ cup	60 mL
Almond flavoring	1 tsp.	5 mL
Icing (confectioner's) sugar		

(continued on next page)

Put flour and butter in large bowl. Cut in butter until crumbly.

Mix sour cream and egg yolks together with a fork to blend. Add to flour mixture. Stir and knead to form ball. Roll out ⅛ inch (3 mm) thick on lightly floured surface. Cut into 2 inch (5 cm) squares.

Filling: Mix almonds, sugar, milk and almond flavoring together. Place ½ tsp. (2 mL) in center of each square. Bring up 2 opposite corners. Lay 1 corner over the other, pinching to seal. Arrange on ungreased baking sheet. Bake in 400°F (200°C) oven for about 10 to 12 minutes until lightly browned.

Roll in icing sugar. Makes 8 dozen.

Pictured on page 125.

THICK WHITE COOKIES

Big cookies, soft and thick. For a variation, sprinkle with granulated sugar before baking.

Butter or margarine, softened	½ cup	125 mL
Granulated sugar	½ cup	125 mL
Brown sugar, packed	½ cup	125 mL
Egg	1	1
Milk	½ cup	125 mL
Vanilla	1 tsp.	5 mL
All–purpose flour	3 cups	750 mL
Cream of tartar	2 tsp.	10 mL
Baking soda	1 tsp.	5 mL
Salt	½ tsp.	2 mL

Cream butter and both sugars together. Beat in egg. Add milk and vanilla.

Stir flour, cream of tartar, baking soda and salt together and add. Mix well. Roll out ¼ inch (6 mm) thick on floured surface. Cut into 2¾ inch (7 cm) rounds. Place on greased baking sheet. Bake in 375°F (190°C) oven for 8 to 10 minutes. Makes 2½ dozen.

Pictured on page 53.

BOILED EGG COOKIES

This is a variation of a popular cookie in Caen. Cooked egg yolks are added to the batter.

Butter or margarine, softened	1 cup	250 mL
Granulated sugar	1 cup	250 mL
Egg yolks	2	2
All–purpose flour	3 cups	750 mL
Hard–boiled eggs, mash yolks and save whites for another purpose	4	4
Egg whites, slightly beaten	2	2
Chopped nuts	¼ cup	60 mL
Granulated sugar	¼ cup	60 mL

Cream butter and first amount of sugar together. Add egg yolks and flour. Mash cooked egg yolks and add to butter mixture. Mix together well. Roll on lightly floured board. Cut into 2 inch (5 cm) rounds. Arrange on ungreased baking sheet.

Brush cookies with egg whites. Mix nuts and remaining sugar together. Sprinkle over top. Bake in 350°F (180°C) oven for 12 to 15 minutes. Makes 6 dozen.

Pictured on page 53.

THICK MOLASSES COOKIES

These big old fashioned cookies are soft and thick.

Cooking oil	1 cup	250 mL
Granulated sugar	1 cup	250 mL
Egg	1	1
Molasses	1 cup	250 mL
Milk	½ cup	125 mL
Baking soda	2 tsp.	10 mL
All–purpose flour	5¼ cups	1.3 L
Salt	½ tsp.	2 mL

(continued on next page)

Beat oil, sugar and egg together well. Add molasses.

Stir milk and baking soda together to dissolve and add.

Add flour and salt. Mix well. Roll out ¼ inch (6 mm) thick on floured surface. Cut into 2¾ inch (7 cm) rounds. Arrange on greased baking sheet. Bake in 375°F (190°C) oven for about 8 to 10 minutes. Makes 3½ dozen.

Pictured on page 35.

CORNMEAL CRISPS

These have the unusual addition of cornmeal. Crispy good.

Butter or margarine, softened	½ cup	125 mL
Granulated sugar	¾ cup	175 mL
Egg	1	1
Lemon juice	2 tsp.	10 mL
Grated lemon rind	1 tsp.	5 mL
All–purpose flour	1½ cups	375 mL
Cornmeal	½ cup	125 mL
Baking powder	1 tsp.	5 mL
Salt	½ tsp.	2 mL
Chopped raisins	½ cup	125 mL

Cream butter and sugar together well. Beat in egg, lemon juice and rind.

Add remaining ingredients. Mix well. Roll out on lightly floured board ¼ inch (6 mm) thick and cut into 2 inch (5 cm) circles. Dough may also be shaped into roll 2 inches (5 cm) in diameter and chilled. Cut into slices ¼ inch (6 mm) thick. Place on greased baking sheet. Bake in 350°F (180°C) oven for 9 to 12 minutes until golden. Makes 3 dozen.

Pictured on page 71.

Paré Pointer

No madam you can't try on that dress in the window. You will have to use a fitting room like everyone else.

RAISIN FILLED COOKIES

Serve hot from the oven for an extra special delight. Dough and filling can be kept refrigerated to bake as needed if desired.

FILLING

Raisins, coarsely chopped	1½ cups	375 mL
Granulated sugar	¾ cup	175 mL
Cornstarch	1 tbsp.	15 mL
Water	¾ cup	175 mL
Lemon juice	1½ tsp.	7 mL

COOKIE DOUGH

Butter or margarine, softened	1 cup	250 mL
Granulated sugar	1½ cups	375 mL
Eggs	2	2
Milk	½ cup	125 mL
Vanilla	1 tsp.	5 mL
All–purpose flour	3½ cups	875 mL
Baking soda	1 tsp.	5 mL
Salt	½ tsp.	2 mL

Granulated sugar for garnish

Filling: Mix all ingredients together in saucepan. Bring to a boil, stirring over medium heat. Cool.

Cookie Dough: Cream butter and sugar together. Beat in eggs 1 at a time. Add milk and vanilla.

Stir flour, baking soda and salt together and add. Mix well. Roll out thinly on floured surface. Cut into 2½ inch (6.5 cm) circles. Arrange circles on greased baking sheet. Drop 1 tsp. (5 mL) raisin filling in center. Cover with second circle. Press edges with floured fork.

Cut a cross in top center about ½ to ¾ inch (1.25 to 2 cm) each way.

Sprinkle with sugar. Bake in 350°F (180°C) oven until lightly browned, about 10 minutes. Makes 4 dozen.

Pictured on page 107.

*Marshmallow halves top chocolate cookie bases then melted choco-
late is drizzled over all.*

Butter or margarine, softened	½ cup	125 mL
Granulated sugar	½ cup	125 mL
Egg	1	1
Sour cream	½ cup	125 mL
Vanilla	½ tsp.	2 mL
All–purpose flour	1¾ cups	425 mL
Cocoa	⅓ cup	75 mL
Baking powder	½ tsp.	2 mL
Baking soda	¼ tsp.	1 mL
Salt	¼ tsp.	1 mL
Large marshmallows, halved	32	32
Semisweet chocolate chips	1 cup	250 mL
Grated parowax (paraffin)	2 tbsp.	30 mL
Butter or margarine	1 tbsp.	15 mL

Cream butter and sugar together in bowl. Beat in egg. Add sour cream
and vanilla. Mix.

Stir flour, cocoa, baking powder, baking soda and salt together. Add
to sour cream mixture. Mix well. On lightly floured surface roll out
dough to ⅛ inch (3 mm) thickness. Cut into 2 inch (5 cm) rounds. Place
on lightly greased baking sheet. Bake in 350°F (180°C) oven for 10 to
12 minutes.

Cut marshmallows in half. Scissors do this well. Place marshmallow
half in center of hot cookie immediately upon removal from oven. Let
stand to cool.

Coating: Melt chocolate chips, wax and butter in small saucepan
over low heat. Spoon over top of marshmallow while holding cookie or
place cookie in sieve over a plate and pour chocolate over top. Place
on waxed paper to set.

Variation: A dab of red jam or half a nut may be hidden underneath
each marshmallow.

Pictured on page 125.

LEBKUCHEN

Layb–COO–cun is a popular well known German Christmas cookie. Leave plain, glaze, or glaze and decorate. Pretty and spicy. No fat in these.

Honey	⅔ cup	150 mL
Molasses	⅓ cup	75 mL
Egg	1	1
Brown sugar, packed	¾ cup	175 mL
Lemon juice	2 tbsp.	30 mL
Chopped candied citron	½ cup	125 mL
Finely chopped almonds	⅓ cup	75 mL
All–purpose flour	3½ cups	800 mL
Cinnamon	1 tsp.	5 mL
Salt	½ tsp.	2 mL
Baking soda	½ tsp.	2 mL
Nutmeg	½ tsp.	2 mL
Cloves	½ tsp.	2 mL

**Flaked almonds, cherries, corn syrup
    for garnish**

Bring honey and molasses to a boil in small saucepan. Remove from heat.

Beat egg in mixing bowl until frothy. Beat in sugar. Add lemon juice, citron, almonds and hot honey–molasses mixture.

Stir next 6 ingredients together and add. Mix well. Roll out ¼ inch (6 mm) thick on floured surface. Cut in 2½ inch (6 cm) circles. Place on greased cookie sheet.

Decorate with flaked almonds and bits of cherries. A dab of corn syrup helps them stick. Bake in 375°F (190°C) oven for about 8 to 10 minutes. Cool. Brush with warm corn syrup to glaze. Makes about 3½ dozen.

Pictured on page 17.

Paré Pointer

They tried to kiss in a dense fog. They mist.

TEETHING BISCUITS

Make your own baby cookies. These are hard and tasty.

Large eggs	2	2
Granulated sugar	1 cup	250 mL
Vanilla	1 tsp.	5 mL
All–purpose flour	2 cups	450 mL

Beat eggs in medium size bowl until frothy. Add sugar, vanilla and 2 cups (450 mL) flour. Mix together. Work in as much remaining flour as you can. Roll ¼ inch (6 mm) thick. Cut into rings and sticks. Place on greased cookie sheet. Let stand uncovered overnight to dry. Next morning bake in 325°F (160°C) oven for about 30 minutes until dry and hard. Cool thoroughly before storing. Makes about 2 dozen.

Pictured on page 89.

WHOLEMEAL WAFERS

A crisp wafer to munch. Not sweet.

Wholewheat flour	2 cups	450 mL
Rolled oats, ground	½ cup	125 mL
Brown sugar, packed	¼ cup	60 mL
Baking powder	1 tsp.	5 mL
Salt	1 tsp.	5 mL
Butter or margarine, softened	½ cup	125 mL
Large Eggs	2	2
Water	2 tbsp.	30 mL

Crumble first 6 ingredients together in bowl until mealy texture.

Put eggs and water into small container. With a fork beat until well mixed. Add to bowl. Mix as for pie crust until it forms a ball. Roll out paper thin on lightly floured surface. Cut into 2½ inch (6.5 cm) circles. Place on greased cookie sheet. Pierce with fork. Bake in 350°F (180°C) oven for about 10 minutes until browned. Makes 6 dozen.

Pictured on page 125.

CANDY CANE COOKIES

A fun cookie for all the family to make together. Reprinted from Company's Coming Holiday Entertaining.

Butter or margarine, softened	1 cup	250 mL
Icing (confectioner's) sugar	1 cup	250 mL
Egg	1	1
Almond flavoring	1 tsp.	5 mL
Vanilla flavoring	1 tsp.	5 mL
Peppermint flavoring	¼ tsp.	1 mL
All–purpose flour	2½ cups	600 mL
Baking powder	1 tsp.	5 mL
Salt	1 tsp.	5 mL
Red food coloring	½ tsp.	2 mL

Mix first 6 ingredients together well.

Add flour, baking powder and salt. Mix well.

Divide dough into 2 equal portions. Add food coloring to 1 portion. Blend well. Roll 1 tsp. (5 mL) of each color dough into ropes about 5½ inches (14 cm) long. Lay them side by side. Pinch ends together. Twist to form a spiral. Lay on ungreased baking sheet. Shape to form a cane. Wreaths are easy to make too. Bake in 350°F (180°C) oven for about 10 minutes until pale gold. Cool on sheet 2 to 3 minutes then remove. Makes about 4½ dozen.

Pictured on page 17.

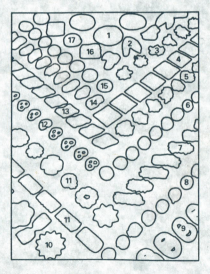

These cookies have the flavor combination of the famous Viennese torte.

Butter or margarine, softened	1 cup	250 mL
Instant chocolate pudding, 4 serving size	1	1
Egg	1	1
All–purpose flour	2 cups	500 mL
Granulated sugar	¼ cup	50 mL
Apricot jam	½ cup	125 mL
Semisweet chocolate chips	½ cup	125 mL
Butter or margarine	3 tbsp.	50 mL

Cream butter and pudding powder together. Beat in egg. Mix in flour. Shape into small balls.

Roll balls in sugar. Place on greased baking sheet. Make a dent in each with your thumb. Bake in 325°F (160°C) oven for 5 minutes. Remove cookies and press dent again. Continue baking for about 10 to 15 minutes.

Fill dents with jam. Melt chocolate and butter in small saucepan over low heat. Stir to hasten melting. Glaze tops of cooled cookies. Makes 4 dozen.

BLACK FOREST COOKIES: Fill with ½ maraschino cherry or with cherry jam instead of apricot.

Pictured on page 143.

Paré Pointer

When the doctor said she had acute angina she said she came to be examined, not admired.

RANGER COOKIES

Chewy and nutritious. Good for snacks, lunch boxes and pockets.

Butter or margarine, softened	**1 cup**	**250 mL**
Granulated sugar	**1 cup**	**250 mL**
Brown sugar	**1 cup**	**250 mL**
Eggs	**2**	**2**
Vanilla	**2 tsp.**	**10 mL**
All–purpose flour	**2 cups**	**500 mL**
Baking soda	**1 tsp.**	**5 mL**
Baking powder	**½ tsp.**	**2 mL**
Salt	**1½ tsp.**	**7 mL**
Crisp rice cereal	**2 cups**	**450 mL**
Rolled oats	**2 cups**	**450 mL**
Coconut	**1 cup**	**225 mL**
Raisins	**1 cup**	**225 mL**

Cream butter and both sugars together. Beat in eggs 1 at a time. Add vanilla.

Stir flour, baking soda, baking powder and salt together and add. Mix.

Add cereal, oats, coconut and raisins. Mix well. Dough will be thick. Roll into 1 inch (2.5 cm) balls or push off pieces of dough from spoon. Arrange on greased baking sheet. Bake in 375°F (190°C) oven for 6 to 8 minutes until golden. Makes 8 dozen.

Pictured on page 125.

You should pay your taxes with a smile. Too bad they insist on cash.

These snaps have crackle tops and a spicy bite to them. An old timer.

Butter or margarine, softened	3/4 cup	175 mL
Granulated sugar	1 cup	250 mL
Egg	1	1
Molasses	1/2 cup	125 mL
All–purpose flour	2 1/2 cups	600 mL
Baking soda	2 tsp.	10 mL
Ginger	2 tsp.	10 mL
Cinnamon	1 tsp.	5 mL
Salt	1/2 tsp.	2 mL
Granulated sugar		

Cream butter and first amount of sugar well. Beat in egg. Mix in molasses.

Stir flour, baking soda, ginger, cinnamon and salt together and add. Mix well. Shape into 1 inch (2.5 cm) balls.

Roll in sugar and place on greased baking sheet. Bake in 350°F (180°C) oven oven for 10 to 12 minutes. Makes 6 dozen.

Pictured on page 71.

Easy to prepare with few ingredients. The result is a tasty crisp cookie. When dipped in chocolate they become tiny chocolate bars.

Butter or margarine, softened	1 cup	250 mL
Granulated sugar	1/2 cup	125 mL
Vanilla	1 tsp.	5 mL
All–purpose flour	2 cups	500 mL
Coconut	1 cup	250 mL

Cream butter, sugar and vanilla well.

Add flour and coconut. Mix together to form a ball. Shape into small balls. Place on greased cookie sheet. Press with fork. Bake in 350°F (180°C) oven for 12 to 15 minutes. Makes 2 1/2 to 3 dozen.

Note: These are extra good dipped in chocolate or glazed with choco–late frosting.

Pictured on page 125.

CHOCOLATE CHIP SHORTBREAD

A scrumptious variation of a popular cookie.

Butter (not margarine), softened	1 cup	250 mL
Brown sugar, packed	½ cup	125 mL
Vanilla	1 tsp.	5 mL
All–purpose flour	2 cups	500 mL
Semisweet chocolate chips	1 cup	250 mL

Measure butter, sugar, vanilla and flour into bowl. Work together until it forms a ball.

Add chocolate chips and work into dough. Roll into 1 inch (2.5 cm) balls. Place on ungreased cookie sheet. Press with fork. Bake in 325° F (160° C) oven for 10 to 15 minutes. Makes 5 dozen.

Pictured on page 89.

LADYFINGERS

Delicate and golden in color. A tea cookie.

Egg whites, room temperature	3	3
Granulated sugar	¼ cup	60 mL
Egg yolks	3	3
Vanilla	1 tsp.	5 mL
Granulated sugar	¼ cup	60 mL
All–purpose flour	⅔ cup	150 mL

In mixing bowl beat egg whites until soft peaks form. Add first amount of sugar gradually, beating until stiff.

In another bowl beat egg yolks, vanilla and second amount of sugar until a light cream color. Fold into egg whites.

Sprinkle flour over top. Fold in. Pipe into strips about ½ x 2½ inches (1.25 x 7.5 cm) onto greased baking sheet. Bake in 350°F (180°C) oven for about 10 minutes. Watch carefully so they don't burn. Makes about 3½ dozen.

Pictured on page 143.

BISCUIT COOKIES

A yummy cookie destined to be in many a lunchbox. Quick to make.

Refrigerated crescent rolls	1 pkg.	1 pkg.
Smooth peanut butter	8 tsp.	40 mL
Granulated sugar	4 tsp.	20 mL
Semisweet chocolate chips	8 tsp.	40 mL
Granulated sugar		

Spread each triangle of dough with 1 tsp. (5 mL) peanut butter. Sprinkle each with ½ tsp. (5 mL) sugar followed by 1 tsp. (5 mL) chocolate chips. Roll from shortest side enclosing all chips as you roll. Roll in sugar and place on ungreased cookie sheet. Bake in 375°F (190°C) oven for 10 to 12 minutes. Makes 8.

Pictured on page 125.

MINT SURPRISE

Bite into this tasty cookie and find a creamy mint hidden inside.

Butter or margarine, softened	½ cup	125 mL
Granulated sugar	½ cup	125 mL
Brown sugar, packed	¼ cup	50 mL
Egg	1	1
Vanilla	½ tsp.	2 mL
All–purpose flour	1½ cups	375 mL
Graham cracker crumbs	¼ cup	50 mL
Baking soda	½ tsp.	2 mL
Salt	½ tsp.	2 mL
Solid mint–flavored chocolate wafers or colored cream mints		

Cream butter and both sugars together. Beat in egg and vanilla.

Add flour, crumbs, baking soda and salt. Mix well.

Wrap each mint in about 1½ tsp. (7 mL) dough. Arrange on ungreased baking sheet. Bake in 375° F (190° C) oven for 8 to 10 minutes until lightly browned. Makes about 5 dozen.

Pictured on page 107.

SPRITZ COOKIES

Put through a cookie press. These are either decorated before baking, left plain or dipped in melted chocolate. Nice and crisp.

Butter or margarine, softened	1 cup	250 mL
Granulated sugar	1 cup	250 mL
Eggs	2	2
Vanilla	1½ tsp.	7 mL
All–purpose flour	3 cups	725 mL
Baking powder	½ tsp.	2 mL
Salt	¼ tsp.	1 mL

Cream butter and sugar together well. Beat in eggs, 1 at a time. Add vanilla.

Stir in flour, baking powder and salt. Force dough through cookie press onto ungreased cookie sheet. Decorate with small colored sugar beads if desired. Bake in 400°F (200°C) oven for about 10 to 12 minutes until edges begin to brown. Makes 6 to 7 dozen.

CHOCOLATE SPRITZ: Exchange 6 tbsp. (100 mL) of flour for an equal amount of cocoa.

ORANGE SPRITZ: Add 2 tsp. (10 mL) grated orange rind and ½ tsp. (2 mL) orange flavoring.

ALMOND SPRITZ: Add 1 tsp. (5 mL) almond flavoring.

CHOCOLATE ORANGE SPRITZ: Exchange 6 tbsp. (100 mL) of flour for an equal amount of cocoa. Add 2 tsp. (10 mL) orange extract. Good.

CHOCOLATE FILLING

Semisweet chocolate chips, melted	⅓ cup	75 mL
Butter or margarine, softened	1 tbsp.	15 mL
Icing (confectioner's) sugar	2 tbsp.	30 mL

Mix all together. Use to sandwich cookies. Makes a scant ½ cup (125 mL).

PEANUT BUTTER FILLING

Smooth peanut butter	¼ cup	60 mL
Butter or margarine, softened	1 tbsp.	15 mL
Icing (confectioner's) sugar	2 tbsp.	30 mL

Mix together well. Spread between 2 thin cookies. Makes a scant ⅓ cup (75 mL).

Pictured on page 107.

Put out a bowlful of these spicy little cookies. Makes a nice snack with coffee. These contain no fat.

Eggs	3	3
Granulated sugar	1 cup	250 mL
Brown sugar, packed	1 cup	250 mL
All–purpose flour	2¾ cups	675 mL
Baking powder	1 tsp.	5 mL
Cinnamon	1 tsp.	5 mL
Allspice	½ tsp.	2 mL
Nutmeg	½ tsp.	2 mL
Cloves	¼ tsp.	1 mL
Pepper, white or black	¼ tsp.	1 mL
Grated lemon rind	1½ tsp.	7 mL
Finely chopped almonds	½ cup	125 mL

In mixing bowl beat eggs until frothy. Add both sugars. Beat until very light and fluffy, at least 5 or 6 minutes.

Add all remaining ingredients. Mix together well. Roll into ropes ½ inch (1.25 cm) in diameter. Slice into pieces ½ inch (1.25 cm) long. Arrange on greased sheet. Bake in 325° F (160° C) oven for 15 minutes until browned. Makes 8 or 9 dozen.

Pictured on page 143.

Paré Pointer

Someone cut a large hole in the fence around the nudist camp. The police are looking into it.

PRETZELS

These are easy to make. A different shape for cookies. Tasty. May be dipped in melted chocolate.

Butter or margarine, softened	½ cup	125 mL
Granulated sugar	½ cup	125 mL
Egg	1	1
Corn syrup	2 tbsp.	30 mL
All–purpose flour	2 cups	500 mL
Baking powder	1 tsp.	5 mL
Salt	⅛ tsp.	0.5 mL

Cream butter and sugar together. Beat in egg. Add corn syrup.

Stir flour, baking powder and salt together and add. Mix well. Shape into 7 inch (17.5 cm) pencil size ropes. Form into a horseshoe. Bring ends down to center of rope overlapping and pressing ends forming pretzel shape. Arrange on greased cookie sheet. These hold their shape much better if chilled for ½ hour or so at this point. Bake in 375°F (190°C) oven for 10 to 12 minutes.

Pictured on page 107.

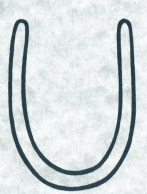

Pretzels

Cloverleaf

Checkerboard

recipes on page 64

WAR-TIME COOKIES

During World War II when sugar was scarce, people were in luck if a pudding powder was available. This is still a favorite today. Not too sweet.

Butterscotch or caramel pudding powder, 4 serving size, not instant	1	1
Butter or margarine, softened	¾ cup	175 mL
Granulated sugar	1 tbsp.	15 mL
All–purpose flour	1 cup	225 mL
Rolled oats	1½ cups	375 mL
Baking powder	¼ tsp.	1 mL
Baking soda	¼ tsp.	1 mL
Salt	⅛ tsp.	0.5 mL
Vanilla	1 tsp.	5 mL
Egg	1	1

In mixing bowl, add and mix ingredients in order given. Roll into balls, 1 to 1¼ inches (2.5 to 3 cm) in diameter. Place on greased baking sheet. Press with fork. Bake in 375° F (190° C) oven for 10 to 15 minutes. Makes about 3 dozen.

Pictured on page 71.

CRACKERJACK COOKIES

Crunchy and good to please any age. A real crackerjack of a cookie.

Butter or margarine, softened	1 cup	250 mL
Brown sugar, packed	1 cup	250 mL
Granulated sugar	1 cup	250 mL
Eggs	2	2
Vanilla	2 tsp.	10 mL
Rolled oats	2 cups	500 mL
Crisp rice cereal	2 cups	500 mL
All–purpose flour	1½ cups	375 mL
Coconut	1 cup	250 mL
Baking powder	1 tsp.	5 mL
Baking soda	1 tsp.	5 mL

Mix first 5 ingredients together well.

Add remaining ingredients. Mix together. Shape into balls. Do not flatten. Arrange on ungreased baking sheet. Bake in 375° F (190° C) oven for 8 to 10 minutes. Makes about 6 dozen.

Pictured on pages 71 and 89.

FORTUNE COOKIES

Making these from scratch enables you to write your own fortune. These are great conversation cookies.

All–purpose flour	¾ **cup**	**175 mL**
Granulated sugar	**1 cup**	**250 mL**
Salt	¼ **tsp.**	**1 mL**
Butter or margarine, melted	½ **cup**	**125 mL**
Egg whites (4 large)	½ **cup**	**125 mL**
Vanilla	**1 tsp.**	**5 mL**

Fortunes typed on paper strips

Stir flour, sugar, and salt together in bowl.

Add remaining ingredients. Beat until smooth. Drop level teaspoonfuls (5 mL) onto greased baking sheet leaving a lot of room for expansion. Bake in 300°F (150°C) oven for 12 to 15 minutes. Fold immediately using tea towel to protect hands from heat. Fold top edges together. Insert fortune on bottom. Have bottom well ballooned apart. Press cookie over thin obect such as side of thin saucepan. Place in muffin tin to ensure they will hold their shape as they cool. Makes 3½ dozen.

Pictured on page 107.

These fragile cookies are baked flat, rolled hot and filled cold. An extra special treat.

Butter or margarine	¼ cup	60 mL
Granulated sugar	¼ cup	60 mL
Corn syrup	2 tbsp.	30 mL
All–purpose flour	½ cup	125 mL
Ginger	½ tsp.	2 mL
Brandy flavoring	1 tsp.	5 mL
Water	4 tsp.	20 mL
FILLING		
Whipping cream	1 cup	250 mL
Granulated sugar	1 tbsp.	15 mL
Brandy flavoring	½ tsp.	2 mL

Put butter, first amount of sugar and syrup in saucepan. Heat and stir until sugar is dissolved.

Remove from heat. Add flour, ginger, brandy flavoring and water. Mix well. Drop by teaspoonfuls onto greased baking sheet allowing room for expansion. Make 4 at once to allow for proper handling. Bake in 350°F (180°C) oven for about 6 to 7 minutes or until edges are golden. Cool 1 minute. Working quickly, loosen 1 cookie. With rough (top) side out, roll around wooden spoon handle to shape. Ease off onto counter. Repeat. If cookies harden too much to remove, put back in oven to heat. These can be kept for a few days or frozen.

Filling: To serve, whip cream, second amount of sugar and brandy flavoring until stiff. Spoon or pipe into rolls. Serve at once. Makes about 16.

Note: To use brandy in cookies omit brandy flavoring and water. Add 2 tbsp. (30 mL) brandy. For filling, omit brandy flavoring and add 1 tbsp. (15 mL) brandy.

Pictured on page 143.

SLOW POKES

Baked long at a low temperature, these cookies shatter and melt in your mouth. A yummy caramel flavor.

Butter or margarine, softened	**1 cup**	**250 mL**
Granulated sugar	**1 cup**	**250 mL**
Egg yolk	**1**	**1**
Vanilla	**2 tsp.**	**10 mL**
All–purpose flour	**2 cups**	**500 mL**
Salt	**¼ tsp.**	**1 mL**
Baking powder	**1 tsp.**	**5 mL**
Hot water	**2 tsp.**	**10 mL**
Baking soda	**1 tsp.**	**5 mL**
Egg white	**1**	**1**
Finely chopped pecans or walnuts	**½ cup**	**125 mL**

Cream butter and sugar together. Add egg yolk and vanilla.

Mix in flour, salt and baking powder. Stir hot water and baking soda together and add. Mix well. Press thinly onto 2 ungreased baking sheets.

Beat egg white until frothy. Brush over top to glaze. Sprinkle with nuts. Bake in 250° F (120° C) oven for 1 hour. Cut into bars 1½ x 2½ inches (4 x 6.5 cm) as soon as they come from the oven. They will crumble if cut when cooled. Makes about 5 dozen.

Pictured on page 17.

He doesn't mind being at the bottom of the class. They teach the same thing at both ends.

Tender little cookies baked in tiny muffin or tart tins. A combination of jam and nuts fill the centers.

Butter or margarine, softened	½ cup	125 mL
Granulated sugar	¾ cup	175 mL
Eggs	2	2
All–purpose flour	2 cups	500 mL
Baking powder	2 tsp.	10 mL
Raspberry jam	1 cup	250 mL
Chopped nuts	½ cup	125 mL

Cream butter and sugar together. Beat in eggs, 1 at a time. Stir in flour and baking powder. Form into round balls, about 36. Place in small greased muffin tins. Press around the edges of each cup.

Mix jam and nuts together. Fill centers with this mixture. Bake in 350° F (180° C) oven for 10 to 15 minutes until edges begin to brown. Makes 3 dozen.

Pictured on page 143.

TEA TIME ROLLS

Crisp and dainty, these are special rolled tea cookies. Good served with ice cream, or may be filled with whipped cream.

Egg whites, room temperature	2	2
Granulated sugar	½ cup	125 mL
All–purpose flour	½ cup	125 mL
Butter or margarine, melted and cooled	¼ cup	60 mL
Grated rind of orange	1	1
Milk	½ cup	125 mL

Beat egg whites until soft peaks form. Gradually beat in sugar until stiff.

Fold in remaining ingredients 1 at a time, in order given. Drop by teaspoonfuls onto greased baking sheet. Make only 4 at a time. Bake in 375°F (190°C) oven for 6 to 7 minutes until browned on edges. Roll while hot around spoon handle or cone shaped object. If cookies harden too quickly, put back in oven to heat. Makes 2½ dozen.

Pictured on page 143.

EASY FIG NEWTONS

Make your own with as much or as little filling as you like. Very tasty.

FILLING

Dried figs, ground	1 lb.	450 g
Water	½ cup	125 mL
Granulated sugar	¼ cup	60 mL
Lemon juice	2 tbsp.	30 mL

DOUGH

Butter or margarine, softened	½ cup	125 mL
Brown sugar, packed	1 cup	250 mL
Eggs	2	2
Vanilla	1 tsp.	5 mL
All–purpose flour	2 cups	500 mL
Baking powder	½ tsp.	2 mL
Baking soda	½ tsp.	2 mL
Salt	½ tsp.	2 mL

Filling: Combine all ingredients in saucepan. Bring to a boil. Simmer for about 5 minutes or so, stirring often. Cool well. Figs may be chopped instead of ground before boiling and then run through blender or food processor before cooling. Add more water if needed.

Dough: Cream butter and sugar together well. Beat in eggs 1 at a time. Add vanilla.

Stir remaining ingredients together and add. Mix well. Divide dough into 2 portions. Chill for about 1 hour. Roll 1 portion thinly on lightly floured surface into rectangle 9 x 15 inches (23 x 37 cm). Using ruler to measure, cut rectangle into 3 long strips each of equal width. Spoon ⅙ of filling down center of each. Fold sides of dough over filling, overlap-ping enough to seal. Place overlapped side down on greased baking sheet. Cut into 1½ inch (4 cm) lengths but do not separate. Bake in 350° F (180° C) oven for 15 to 20 minutes until lightly browned. Cut through to bottom again between each cookie, then remove from baking sheet. Makes 5 dozen.

Pictured on page 89.

MOLASSES ROLLS

Crisp dark–colored cookies that are rolled after baking. These are tasty left plain but may also be filled with whipped cream.

Butter or margarine	¼ cup	60 mL
Granulated sugar	½ cup	125 mL
Table molasses	¾ cup	175 mL
All–purpose flour	1 cup	250 mL
Salt	¾ tsp.	3 mL

Melt butter in saucepan. Add sugar and molasses. Stir and bring to a boil. Cool for about 5 minutes.

Stir in flour and salt. Drop by teaspoonfuls onto greased baking sheet. Bake in 350°F (180°C) oven for 8 to 9 minutes. Watch carefully. These darken very fast. As soon as cookie can be removed from sheet, about 1 minute, roll around finger or spoon handle. If they harden before you finish rolling them, put back in oven to heat. Bake only 4 at a time for easy handling. Makes about 3½ dozen.

Pictured on page 53.

BUTTER THINS

Buttery rich, these resemble little saddles.

Butter, softened	¼ cup	60 mL
Granulated sugar	½ cup	125 mL
Vanilla	½ tsp.	2 mL
Egg white	1	1
All–purpose flour	⅓ cup	75 mL

Cream butter and sugar together. Stir in vanilla, egg white and flour. Drop 1½ teaspoonfuls (7 mL) onto greased baking sheet. Make only 4 at a time. Bake in 350°F (180°C) oven for 5 to 6 minutes. Let stand on baking sheet for about 1 minute. Remove and press gently over rolling pin to shape. Makes about 20.

Pictured on page 125.

CHOCOLATE WALNUT LOGS

These perky little chocolate logs have one end coated in nuts.

Butter or margarine, softened	½ cup	125 mL
Granulated sugar	¼ cup	50 mL
Cocoa	2 tbsp.	30 mL
Vanilla	1 tsp.	5 mL
Salt	⅛ tsp.	0.5 mL
Egg yolk	1	1
All–purpose flour	1 cup	250 mL
COATING		
Egg white, lightly beaten	1	1
Finely chopped walnuts	¼ cup	50 mL
Granulated sugar	2 tbsp.	30 mL

Measure first 6 ingredients into mixing bowl. Beat until fluffy.

Stir in flour. Roll into ropes. Cut into 2 inch (5 cm) lengths.

Coating: Dip 1 end of each log in egg white, then in mixture of nuts and sugar. Arrange on greased baking sheet about 1 inch (2.5 cm) apart. Bake in 350°F (180°C) oven for about 15 minutes. Makes 4 dozen.

Pictured on page 17.

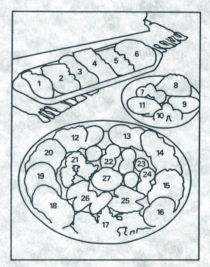

These tender little balls melt in your mouth. They are sometimes known as Mexican Wedding Cakes or Russian Tea Cakes. Reprinted from Company's Coming Holiday Entertaining.

Butter or margarine, softened	1 cup	250 mL
Icing (confectioner's) sugar	½ cup	125 mL
All–purpose flour	2¼ cups	550 mL
Ground pecans	1 cup	250 mL
Vanilla	2 tsp.	10 mL
Icing (confectioner's) sugar	½ cup	125 mL

Combine first 5 ingredients in bowl. Mix first with spoon then by hand to work it until it holds together. Shape into 1 inch (2.5 cm) balls. Arrange on ungreased baking sheet. Bake in 325°F (160°C) oven for 20 to 25 minutes.

As soon as balls have cooled enough to handle, roll them in icing sugar. Makes about 6 dozen.

ALMOND BALLS: Omit pecans. Add 1 cup (250 mL) ground almonds.

ALMOND CRESCENTS: Omit pecans. Add 2 cups (500 mL) ground almonds. Roll into ropes as thick as your finger. Cut into 2 inch (5 cm) lengths. Pinch ends to taper. Shape into crescents.

BURIED CHERRY: Completely cover well drained maraschino cher–ries with dough. Bake same as above.

Pictured on page 17.

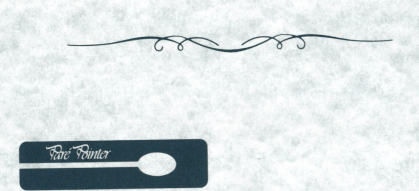

Paré Pointer

A suitable greeting for a bird with webbed feet would be "What's up, duck?"

DOUBLE CHOCOLATE CHIPPERS

These are a chocoholic's delight.

Eggs	4	4
Granulated sugar	1¾ cup	400 mL
Cooking oil	1 cup	225 mL
Unsweetened chocolate squares, melted	4 x 1 oz.	4 x 28 g
Vanilla	1 tsp.	5 mL
All–purpose flour	3¾ cups	850 mL
Baking powder	2 tsp.	10 mL
Salt	¼ tsp.	1 mL
Semisweet chocolate chips	1 cup	250 mL
Icing (confectioner's) sugar	1 cup	250 mL

Beat eggs until frothy. Add sugar and beat. Mix in cooking oil, chocolate and vanilla.

Add flour, baking powder, salt and chips. Stir to mix. Roll into 1 inch (2.5 cm) balls and then into icing sugar, if desired. Place on greased sheet. Bake in 350°F (180°C) oven for 8 to 10 minutes. Do not overbake. Makes 6 dozen.

Pictured on page 53.

POTATO CHIP COOKIES

Try your chips in a cookie instead of using with a dip.

Butter or margarine, softened	½ cup	125 mL
Granulated sugar	½ cup	125 mL
Brown sugar, packed	½ cup	125 mL
Egg	1	1
Vanilla	½ tsp.	2 mL
All–purpose flour	1 cup	250 mL
Baking soda	½ tsp.	2 mL
Crushed potato chips	1 cup	250 mL
Chopped pecans	½ cup	125 mL

Cream butter and both sugars together well. Beat in egg and vanilla.

Add remaining ingredients. Mix well. Roll into 1 inch (2.5 cm) balls. Place on ungreased baking sheet. Leave as is or flatten with glass dipped in granulated sugar. Bake in 350°F (180°C) oven for 10 to 12 minutes. Makes 3 dozen.

Pictured on page 71.

ANGEL COOKIES

A light crisp cookie perfect for tea.

Butter or margarine, softened	1 cup	250 mL
Granulated sugar	½ cup	125 mL
Brown sugar, packed	½ cup	125 mL
Egg	1	1
Vanilla	1 tsp.	5 mL
All–purpose flour	2 cups	500 mL
Cream of tartar	1 tsp.	5 mL
Baking soda	1 tsp.	5 mL
Salt	¼ tsp.	1 mL

Cream butter and both sugars together well. Beat in egg and vanilla.

Stir remaining ingredients together and add. Mix. Shape into 1 inch (2.5 cm) balls. Arrange on ungreased cookie sheet. Press with fork. Bake in 350°F (180°C) oven for 8 to 10 minutes until golden. Makes 5 dozen.

Variation: Add cherries, nuts, chocolate chips or raisins.

Pictured on page 143.

CHOCOLATE SNAPS

These resemble ginger snaps in appearance. Crisp enough for dunk–ing.

Eggs	2	2
Butter or margarine, softened	½ cup	125 mL
Chocolate cake mix, 2 layer size, (Devil's food is best)	1	1
Icing (confectioner's) sugar or granulated sugar (optional)		

Beat eggs with spoon. Add butter and cake mix. Stir together well. Shape into 1 inch (2.5 cm) balls. Roll in sugar if desired. Place on greased cookie sheet. Bake in 375° F (190° C) oven for 8 to 10 minutes. Let stand 1 minute. Remove to cool on racks. Makes about 4 dozen.

Pictured on page 53.

JAM DIAGONALS

Pretty as a picture. Saves time by baking in strips and cutting into cookies before cooling.

Butter or margarine, softened	1 cup	250 mL
Granulated sugar	1/2 cup	125 mL
Egg	1	1
Vanilla	1 tsp.	5 mL
Lemon flavoring	1/4 tsp.	1 mL
All–purpose flour	2 1/2 cups	625 mL
Baking powder	1/2 tsp.	2 mL
Salt	1/4 tsp.	1 mL
Raspberry jam, sieved	1/3 cup	75 mL

Cream butter and sugar in bowl. Beat in egg, vanilla and lemon flavoring.

Stir flour, baking powder and salt together. Add and mix. Divide dough into 8 portions. Make each into a rope about 10 inches (25 cm) long and 3/4 inch (2 cm) wide. Place on ungreased baking sheet. With side of your hand, press to indent along center lengthwise of each strip.

Spread seedless raspberry jam in indentations. Bake in 350°F (180°C) oven for 15 to 17 minutes. Cut while warm into 1 inch (2.5 cm) diagonal slices. Makes about 5 dozen.

Pictured on page 107.

ANISE DROPS

These moist drops have a mild licorice flavor to them. Pleasant and different.

Butter or margarine, softened	1/4 cup	60 mL
Granulated sugar	3/4 cup	175 mL
Eggs	2	2
Aniseed	2 tbsp.	30 mL
Grated lemon rind	1 tsp.	5 mL
All–purpose flour	2 cups	500 mL
Baking powder	1 tbsp.	15 mL
Salt	1/2 tsp.	2 mL

(continued on next page)

Cream butter and sugar together. Beat in eggs 1 at a time. Stir in aniseed and lemon rind.

Stir flour, baking powder and salt together and add. Mix well. Shape into 1 inch (2.5 cm) balls. Place on greased cookie sheet. Press with floured fork. Bake in 375°F (190°C) oven for 8 to 10 minutes. Glaze. Makes 3 dozen.

GLAZE: Mix lemon juice with 1 cup (250 mL) icing (confectioner's) sugar to make barely pourable glaze. Spoon over cookies allowing some to run down sides.

Pictured on page 53.

CHOCOLATE CRINKLES

Rolled in powdered sugar and baked in small balls, these cookies turn out crackly and white.

Butter or margarine, softened	¼ cup	60 mL
Granulated sugar	2 cups	500 mL
Eggs	3	3
Vanilla	2 tsp.	10 mL
Unsweetened chocolate squares, melted	4 x 1 oz.	4 x 28 g
All–purpose flour	2½ cups	575 mL
Baking powder	2 tsp.	10 mL
Salt	½ tsp.	2 mL
Icing (confectioner's) sugar	1 cup	250 mL

Cream butter and sugar together. Beat in eggs, 1 at a time. Mix in vanilla and chocolate.

Stir flour, baking powder and salt together. Add and mix well. Shape into 1 inch (2.5 cm) balls.

Roll balls in icing sugar. Coat well. Arrange on greased baking sheet. Bake in 350° F (180° C) oven for 8 to 12 minutes. Cookies will be soft. Makes 6 dozen.

Pictured on page 35.

POP'S COOKIES

Light and crunchy. Excellent choice.

Butter or margarine, softened	1 cup	250 mL
Granulated sugar	1 cup	250 mL
Brown sugar, packed	1/2 cup	125 mL
Egg	1	1
Vanilla	1 tsp.	5 mL
Shredded wheat biscuits, crushed	2	2
Rolled oats	1 1/2 cups	375 mL
All–purpose flour	1 1/2 cups	375 mL
Baking powder	1 tsp.	5 mL
Baking soda	1 tsp.	5 mL

In mixing bowl, cream butter and both sugars together well. Beat in egg and vanilla.

Add crushed shredded wheat — measures 2/3 cup (150 mL) — and rolled oats. Stir flour, baking powder and baking soda together and add. Mix. Roll into 1 inch (2.5 cm) balls. Place on greased baking sheet. Flatten with fork. If fork sticks, dip in flour. Bake in 375°F (190°C) oven for 8 to 10 minutes until lightly browned. Makes about 6 dozen.

Pictured on page 71.

TURTLE COOKIES

Snappy and cute. A birthday party special.

Butter or margarine, softened	1/2 cup	125 mL
Brown sugar, packed	1/2 cup	125 mL
Egg	1	1
Egg yolk	1	1
Vanilla	1/4 tsp.	1 mL
Maple flavoring	1/8 tsp.	0.5 mL
All–purpose flour	1 1/2 cups	375 mL
Baking soda	1/4 tsp.	1 mL
Salt	1/4 tsp.	1 mL
Egg white, fork beaten	1	1
Pecan halves, split	1 1/2 cups	375 mL
Semisweet chocolate chips		

(continued on next page)

Cream butter and sugar together. Beat in egg, yolk and flavorings.

Stir in flour, baking soda and salt. Shape into 1 inch (2.5 cm) balls.

Place 3 nut pieces on greased cookie sheet to form head and 2 front legs plus 2 pieces for back legs.

Dip bottom of ball into egg white. Place in center of shaped nuts. Flatten slightly. Bake in 350°F (180°C) oven for 10 to 12 minutes. Cool.

Place 6 to 8 semisweet chocolate chips on each hot cookie. Allow them to melt, then spread with knife. Chocolate icing may be used as an alternative. Makes 3½ dozen.

Pictured on page 35.

CHERRY WINKS

A combination of cereal, fruit and nuts produces a pretty party cookie.

Butter or margarine, softened	¾ cup	175 mL
Granulated sugar	1 cup	250 mL
Eggs	2	2
All–purpose flour	2 cups	450 mL
Baking powder	1 tsp.	5 mL
Baking soda	½ tsp.	2 mL
Salt	½ tsp.	2 mL
Chopped pecans or walnuts	1 cup	250 mL
Chopped dates or raisins	1 cup	250 mL
Cornflakes or other cereal flakes	3 cups	750 mL
Maraschino cherries, halved or quartered, blotted dry	15–30	15–30

Cream butter and sugar together in bowl. Beat in eggs.

Stir flour, baking powder, baking soda and salt together and add along with nuts and dates. Mix well. Shape into small balls.

Crush cornflakes into crumbs. Roll balls in crumbs. Place on greased baking sheet. Top with half or quarter cherry. Bake in 350° F (180° C) oven for 10 to 12 minutes. Makes 4 to 5 dozen.

Pictured on page 17.

FATTIGMAN

A Scandinavian Christmas cookie that is deep fried. It makes a large batch that keeps for months in the freezer.

Whipping cream	½ cup	125 mL
Eggs	2	2
Egg yolks	3	3
Granulated sugar	½ cup	125 mL
Butter or margarine, softened	¼ cup	60 mL
Brandy (or use 1½ tsp., 7 mL brandy flavoring plus water)	3 tbsp.	45 mL
Cardamom	½ tsp.	2 mL
All–purpose flour	2½ cups	625 mL

Fat for deep–frying
Icing (confectioner's) sugar for dusting

In small bowl beat cream until stiff. Set aside.

Using same beaters beat eggs and yolks in large mixing bowl until frothy. Add sugar and beat well. Beat in butter. Add brandy, cardamom and whipping cream. Stir.

Add flour. Stir. Let batter stand in refrigerator overnight. Next day roll thinly. Cut into diamond shapes 2 x 5 inches (5 x 15 cm). Cut slit in center. Pull 1 end through slit or leave flat.

Deep–fry a few at a time in hot fat 375° F (190° C). Drain on paper towel. These are sweet enough to serve plain. Dust with icing sugar if desired. Makes about 8 dozen.

Pictured on page 17.

Paré Pointer

A common greeting from the rake in the garden — "Hi, hoe!"

PEANUT OATMEAL COOKIES

Chewy peanut butter flavored treats for everyone.

Butter or margarine, softened	½ cup	125 mL
Brown sugar, packed	1 cup	250 mL
Egg	1	1
Vanilla	½ tsp.	2 mL
Smooth peanut butter	½ cup	125 mL
Rolled oats	2 cups	500 mL
Whole wheat flour (or all–purpose)	½ cup	125 mL
Baking powder	½ tsp.	2 mL
Baking soda	½ tsp.	2 mL
Salt	¼ tsp.	1 mL

Cream butter and sugar together. Beat in egg. Add vanilla and peanut butter.

Mix in remaining ingredients. Shape into small balls or drop by spoon–fuls onto ungreased cookie sheet allowing room for expansion. Bake in 375°F (190°C) oven for 12 to 15 minutes. Makes about 3 dozen.

Pictured on page 53.

HEDGE HOGS

Soft and chewy. A snap to make.

Butter or margarine, melted	2 tbsp.	30 mL
Brown sugar, packed	1 cup	250 mL
Chopped walnuts	2 cups	500 mL
Chopped dates	2 cups	500 mL
All–purpose flour	½ cup	125 mL
Vanilla	2 tsp.	10 mL
Eggs	2	2

Coconut, shredded or medium

Measure first 7 ingredients into bowl. Mix together well. Shape into small balls.

Roll balls in coconut. Place on greased baking sheet. Bake in 350°F (180°C) oven for 10 to 12 minutes. Makes about 3½ dozen.

Pictured on page 35.

CHINESE ALMOND COOKIES

To obtain the true flavor for these cookies, lard is required.

Lard, room temperature	1 cup	250 mL
Granulated sugar	1 cup	250 mL
Egg	1	1
Almond flavoring	2 tsp.	10 mL
All–purpose flour	2½ cups	625 mL
Baking powder	1 tsp.	5 mL
Salt	1 tsp.	5 mL
Blanched almonds	48	48
Egg	1	1
Water	1 tbsp.	15 mL

In mixing bowl, cream lard and sugar. Beat in 1 egg and almond flavoring.

Stir flour, baking powder and salt together and add. Mix. Roll into 48 balls. Arrange on lightly greased baking sheets.

Place whole almond in center. Press with glass to flatten ball some– what. Beat 1 egg white with water. Brush egg and water mixture over cookies. Bake in 350°F (180°C) oven for 8 to 12 minutes until lightly browned. Makes 4 dozen.

Pictured on page 53.

LEMON CRACKS

These golden cookies have real lemon flavor. Refreshing.

Butter or margarine, softened	½ cup	125 mL
Granulated sugar	¼ cup	50 mL
Brown sugar, packed	½ cup	125 mL
Egg	1	1
Grated lemon rind	1 tbsp.	15 mL
Lemon juice	2 tbsp.	30 mL
All–purpose flour	1½ cups	375 mL
Baking powder	1 tsp.	5 mL
Baking soda	½ tsp.	2 mL
Granulated sugar		

(continued on next page)

Cream butter and next 2 sugars. Beat in egg. Add lemon rind and juice.

Stir flour, baking powder and baking soda together and add. Mix well. Shape into balls. Roll in sugar. Place on ungreased sheet. Bake in 350° F (180° C) oven for 10 to 15 minutes. Makes 4 dozen.

Variation: Add 2 cups (500 mL) raisins.

Pictured on page 53.

COOKIE CAPS

These are topped with meringue before baking. They freeze well. A different cookie.

Butter or margarine, softened	**½ cup**	**125 mL**
Granulated sugar	**½ cup**	**125 mL**
Egg	**1**	**1**
Milk	**2 tbsp.**	**30 mL**
All–purpose flour	**1½ cups**	**375 mL**
Baking powder	**½ tsp.**	**2 mL**
MERINGUE TOPPING		
Egg white, room temperature	**1**	**1**
Cream of tartar	**⅛ tsp.**	**0.5 mL**
Brown or granulated sugar	**2 tbsp.**	**30 mL**
Vanilla	**½ tsp.**	**2 mL**
Semisweet chocolate chips	**½ cup**	**125 mL**

Cream butter and sugar. Beat in egg and milk.

Add flour and baking powder. Stir. Shape into small balls. Place on ungreased pan. Flatten with sugared glass.

Meringue Topping: Beat egg white and cream of tartar until soft peaks form. Add sugar in 2 additions beating until stiff. Fold in vanilla and chips. Put a dab on top of each cookie. Bake in 325°F (160°C) oven for 15 to 20 minutes. Makes about 3 dozen.

Pictured on page 125.

PEANUT BLOSSOMS

These really do look like blossoms.

All–purpose flour	1¾ cups	425 mL
Granulated sugar	½ cup	125 mL
Brown sugar, packed	½ cup	125 mL
Baking soda	1 tsp.	5 mL
Salt	½ tsp.	2 mL
Egg	1	1
Butter or margarine, softened	½ cup	125 mL
Smooth peanut butter	½ cup	125 mL
Milk	2 tbsp.	30 mL
Vanilla	1 tsp.	5 mL
Granulated sugar	⅓ cup	75 mL
Chocolate buds or kisses	72	72

Measure first 10 ingredients into mixing bowl. Beat on low speed until a dough forms. Shape into small 1 inch (2.5 cm) balls.

Roll in sugar and place on ungreased cookie sheet. Do not press down. Bake in 375° F (190° C) oven for 10 to 12 minutes.

Top with a chocolate kiss immediately. Press down until cookie cracks around the edges. Makes about 6 dozen.

Pictured on page 53.

Paré Pointer

The man who supplies a pickle factory with cucumbers is the farmer in the dill.

PEANUT BUTTER COOKIES

Makes a huge batch but can easily be halved. Certain children have been raised on these. A family favorite. One serving is as many as can be held between thumb and index finger.

Butter or margarine, softened	1 cup	250 mL
Brown sugar, packed	1 cup	250 mL
Granulated sugar	1 cup	250 mL
Eggs	2	2
Smooth peanut butter	1 cup	250 mL
All–purpose flour	3 cups	750 mL
Baking soda	2 tsp.	10 mL
Salt	1/4 tsp.	1 mL

Cream butter and both sugars together. Beat in eggs, 1 at a time. Mix in peanut butter.

Stir in flour, baking soda and salt. Shape into small balls. Place on ungreased cookie sheets allowing room for expansion. Press with fork. Dip fork in flour as needed to prevent batter stickiness. Bake in 375°F (190°C) oven for 12 to 15 minutes. Makes 6 dozen. See page 92 to make lollipops.

PEANUT BUTTER CHIP COOKIES: Add 1 to 2 cups (250–500 mL) semisweet chocolate chips.

PEANUT BUTTER JELLY NESTS: Shape dough into 1 inch (2.5 cm) balls. Place on cookie sheet. Press with thumb to indent. Bake in 375°F (190°C) oven for 5 minutes. Press again. Bake for 7 to 10 minutes more. Fill with red raspberry or strawberry jelly while cookies are still warm or store and fill as needed.

Pictured on cover.

LOLLIPOPS: To make peanut butter lollipops see method for Rolled Ginger Cookies on page 93.

Paré Pointer

Of course a sneeze is usually pointed Atchoo!

LEMON PIE COOKIES

A crisp cookie just right for dunking. A lemon pie filling is used for these.

Butter or margarine, softened	1 cup	250 mL
Brown sugar, packed	½ cup	125 mL
Lemon pudding and pie filling mix, 1 pie size, not instant	1	1
Water	1 tbsp.	15 mL
All–purpose flour	2 cups	500 mL
Chopped walnuts	½ cup	125 mL

Cream butter and sugar together. Mix in dry pie filling and water.

Add flour and nuts. Mix well. Shape into 1 inch (2.5 cm) balls. Place on ungreased baking sheet. Leave some as is. Press others with fork. Bake in 325°F (160°C) oven for 12 to 15 minutes until golden. While hot, dip into Lemon Dip. Makes about 5 dozen.

LEMON DIP: Put 3 tbsp. (45 mL) lemon juice and ¼ cup (60 mL) granulated sugar into small saucepan. Heat and stir to dissolve. Dip cookie tops. Let stand to dry.

Pictured on page 53.

COCO RUM DIAGONALS

Coconut flavored cookies topped with rum icing.

Butter or margarine, softened	½ cup	125 mL
Granulated sugar	¼ cup	50 mL
Vanilla	1 tsp.	5 mL
Salt	⅛ tsp.	0.5 mL
All–purpose flour	1 cup	250 mL
Baking powder	½ tsp.	2 mL
Flaked coconut	1 cup	250 mL
ICING		
Icing (confectioner's) sugar	1 cup	250 mL
Water	1½ tbsp.	25 mL
Rum flavoring	½ tsp.	2 mL

(continued on next page)

Measure first 4 ingredients into bowl. Beat until fluffy.

Stir flour and baking powder together. Add along wtih coconut. Mix. Make 6 ropes, 9 inches (23 cm) long. Place on greased baking sheet. Bake in 350°F (180°C) oven for 18 to 20 minutes. Ice while warm.

Icing: Mix all 3 ingredients together. Add more water or icing sugar to make proper spreading consistency. Ice strips while slightly warm. Cut into 1 inch (2.5 cm) diagonals.

Pictured on page 125.

CHERRY SURPRISE

These chocolate covered cherries are a popular flavor combination.

Butter or margarine, softened	½ cup	125 mL
Granulated sugar	1 cup	250 mL
Cocoa, sifted	¼ cup	60 mL
Egg	1	1
All–purpose flour	1 cup	250 mL
Salt	⅛ tsp.	0.5 mL
Chopped walnuts	½ cup	125 mL
Maraschino cherries, well drained	48	48

In mixing bowl, cream butter and sugar together with spoon. Stir in cocoa. Add egg and beat with spoon.

Stir in flour, salt and nuts. Chill for 30 minutes.

Blot cherries dry with paper towels. Pinch off small piece of dough. Flatten with fingers and wrap around cherry to enclose completely. Place on ungreased cookie sheet. Bake in 375°F (190°C) oven for 10 to 12 minutes. Glaze. Makes 4 dozen.

GLAZE: Stir enough maraschino cherry juice into 1 cup (250 mL) icing (confectioner's) sugar to make a barely pourable glaze. Dip cookies or spoon over top. Allow to dry.

CHOCOLATE MINT SURPRISE: Wrap dough around solid chocolate wafer that has a mint flavor.

Pictured on page 35.

SESAME SNACKERS

Excellent nutty flavor to these.

Cooking oil	¾ cup	175 mL
Brown sugar, packed	1½ cups	375 mL
Egg	1	1
Vanilla	1 tsp.	5 mL
All–purpose flour	2 cups	450 mL
Baking powder	1 tsp.	5 mL
Salt	¼ tsp.	1 mL
Sesame seeds, toasted in 350°F (180°C) oven for 10 to 15 minutes to brown, stirring twice	½ cup	125 mL

Toasted sesame seeds for topping

Combine cooking oil, sugar, egg and vanilla in mixing bowl. Beat well.

Add flour, baking powder, salt and first amount of sesame seeds. Stir well. Shape into small balls. Place on ungreased baking sheet. Flatten with glass.

Sprinkle with sesame seeds. Bake in 350° F (180° C) oven for 8 to 10 minutes. Makes 4 dozen.

Pictured on page 89.

The aroma of these baking will bring everyone to the kitchen for some samples.

Butter or margarine, softened	1 cup	250 mL
Granulated sugar	1½ cups	375 mL
Eggs	2	2
All–purpose flour	2½ cups	625 mL
Cream of tartar	2 tsp.	10 mL
Baking soda	1 tsp.	5 mL
Salt	¼ tsp.	1 mL
Granulated sugar	2 tbsp.	30 mL
Cinnamon	2 tsp.	10 mL

Cream butter and first amount of sugar well. Beat in eggs 1 at a time.

Mix in flour, cream of tartar, baking soda and salt. Shape into 1 inch (2.5 cm) balls.

Stir remaining sugar and cinnamon together in small dish. Roll balls in mixture to coat. Place on ungreased cookie sheet. Bake in 400° F (200° C) oven for 7 to 8 minutes. Makes about 4 dozen.

Pictured on page 35.

Paré Pointer

Johnny fed the cat pennies when his mother told him to put something in the kitty.

ROSETTES

A crisp deep–fried Scandinavian cookie that is not too sweet. Made with a rosette iron.

Eggs	2	2
Granulated sugar	1 tbsp.	15 mL
Milk	1 cup	250 mL
All–purpose flour	1 cup	250 mL
Salt	1/2 tsp.	2 mL
Fat for deep–frying		

Beat eggs with a spoon in mixing bowl. Add sugar and milk. Stir in flour and salt mixing until smooth.

Heat rosette iron in hot fat 375°F (190°C) for about 1 minute. Dip into batter almost to the top (not over) of the mold. Immerse in hot fat completely covering mold. Fry until golden, about 25 to 35 seconds. Bubbles almost will have stopped. Gently push cookie off rosette. Place upside down on waxed paper to drain. May be frozen at this point. To serve, sprinkle with icing (confectioner's) sugar. Makes 3 to 3½ dozen.

Pictured on page 143.

MELTING MOMENTS

These small delicate cookies are attractive when sandwiched with tinted icing. A cherry turns a "drop" into a festive treat.

Butter (not margarine), softened	1 cup	250 mL
Icing (confectioner's) sugar	1/3 cup	75 mL
Vanilla	1 tsp.	5 mL
All–purpose flour	1½ cups	375 mL
Cornstarch	1/2 cup	125 mL

Mix together well. Knead to form ball of dough. Pinch off small pieces of dough. Place on ungreased cookie sheet. If you prefer, roll into 1 inch (2.5 cm) balls. Press with fork or glass. Bake in 325°F (160°C) oven for 12 to 15 minutes. Sandwich together with colored icing or serve plain. Makes 5 dozen.

Variation: Drop by spoonfuls onto baking sheet. Press cherry or pecan halves into centers.

Pictured on page 17.

A bite into these and you discover a date and nut center.

Chopped walnuts	1 cup	250 mL
Chopped dates	1 cup	250 mL
Lemon juice	2 tsp.	10 mL
Butter or margarine, softened	½ cup	125 mL
Granulated sugar	½ cup	125 mL
Eggs, beaten	2	2
All–purpose flour	2 cups	500 mL
Baking powder	1 tsp.	5 mL

Granulated sugar for garnish

Put walnuts and dates through grinder or food processor. Mix with lemon juice. Form into marble–size balls, about 60.

Cream butter and sugar together. Add beaten eggs.

Stir flour and baking powder together and add. Mix well. Roll into 60 small balls. Flatten each and wrap around marble balls. Place on ungreased baking sheet. Sprinkle (or dip) tops with granulated sugar. Bake in 350°F (180°C) oven until light brown, about 15 minutes. Makes 5 dozen.

Pictured on page 35.

Paré Pointer

Cross a parrot and a woodpecker and you will get a bird that talks in Morse code.

SWEDISH TEA CAKES

You will need to double this recipe. Also known as Swedish Pastry and Thumbprints.

Butter or margarine, softened	½ cup	125 mL
Brown sugar, packed	¼ cup	50 mL
Egg yolk	1	1
All–purpose flour	1 cup	250 mL
Baking powder	½ tsp.	2 mL
Salt	⅛ tsp.	0.5 mL
Egg white, fork beaten	1	1
Finely chopped nuts for coating	⅔ cup	150 mL
Jam or jelly (red is best)		

Cream butter and sugar together. Beat in egg yolk.

Stir flour, baking powder and salt together and add. Mix. Shape into small balls.

Dip into egg white, roll in nuts and place on greased baking sheet. Dent each with your thumb. Bake in 325°F (160°C) oven for 5 minutes. Remove and press dents again. Continue to bake for 10 to 15 minutes until golden brown.

Fill dents with jam while warm, or store unfilled to be filled as used. Makes about 20.

Pictured on page 17.

A midget's greeting "Small world, isn't it?"

These brown caramelized cookies add to any tray of goodies. Some–times known as Palm Leaves, this is puff pastry at its best.

Frozen puff pastry, thawed   **14 oz.**   **397 g**
Icing (confectioner's) sugar or
   granulated

Generously sprinkle counter with sugar. Roll half of the pastry at a time to a long rectangle 6 x 12 inches (15 x 30 cm) in size. Using a pastry brush dipped in water moisten the surface very slightly. Roll each long side to meet in center. Press rolls together lightly. Wrap in plastic or waxed paper and chill thoroughly.

To bake, cut into slices ¼ inch (6 mm) thick. Dip cut sides into sugar on counter. Place on greased baking sheet allowing room for expansion. Bake in 400°F (200°C) oven for about 10 minutes until a rich car–amelized brown. These must be turned over halfway through baking to brown evenly on both sides. Makes 5 dozen.

PUFF BALLS: Roll pastry ¼ inch (6 mm) thick. Cut into 2 inch (5 cm) rounds. Dip in granulated sugar and place on greased baking sheet. These must be turned over halfway through baking. Bake in 375°F (190°C) oven for about 10 minutes. Makes 5 dozen.

Pictured on page 53.

Paré Pointer

When bankers dance, they do the vaults.

METRIC CONVERSION

Throughout this book measurements are given in Conventional and Metric measure. To compensate for differences between the two measurements due to rounding, a full metric measure is not always used. The cup used is the standard 8 fluid ounce. Temperature is given in degrees Fahrenheit and Celsius. Baking pan measurements are in inches and centimetres as well as quarts and litres. An exact metric conversion is given below as well as the working equivalent (Standard Measure).

OVEN TEMPERATURES

Fahrenheit (°F)	Celsius (°C)
175°	80°
200°	95°
225°	110°
250°	120°
275°	140°
300°	150°
325°	160°
350°	175°
375°	190°
400°	205°
425°	220°
450°	230°
475°	240°
500°	260°

SPOONS

Conventional Measure	Metric Exact Conversion Millilitre (mL)	Metric Standard Measure Millilitre (mL)
1/4 teaspoon (tsp.)	1.2 mL	1 mL
1/2 teaspoon (tsp.)	2.4 mL	2 mL
1 teaspoon (tsp.)	4.7 mL	5 mL
2 teaspoons (tsp.)	9.4 mL	10 mL
1 tablespoon (tbsp.)	14.2 mL	15 mL

CUPS

1/4 cup (4 tbsp.)	56.8 mL	50 mL
1/3 cup (5 1/3 tbsp.)	75.6 mL	75 mL
1/2 cup (8 tbsp.)	113.7 mL	125 mL
2/3 cup (10 2/3 tbsp.)	151.2 mL	150 mL
3/4 cup (12 tbsp.)	170.5 mL	175 mL
1 cup (16 tbsp.)	227.3 mL	250 mL
4 1/2 cups	1022.9 mL	1000 mL (1 L)

DRY MEASUREMENTS

Ounces (oz.)	Grams (g)	Grams (g)
1 oz.	28.3 g	30 g
2 oz.	56.7 g	55 g
3 oz.	85.0 g	85 g
4 oz.	113.4 g	125 g
5 oz.	141.7 g	140 g
6 oz.	170.1 g	170 g
7 oz.	198.4 g	200 g
8 oz.	226.8 g	250 g
16 oz.	453.6 g	500 g
32 oz.	907.2 g	1000 g (1 kg)

PANS, CASSEROLES

Conventional Inches	Metric Centimetres	Conventional Quart (qt.)	Metric Litre (L)
8x8 inch	20x20 cm	1 2/3 qt.	2 L
9x9 inch	22x22 cm	2 qt.	2.5 L
9x13 inch	22x33 cm	3 1/3 qt.	4 L
10x15 inch	25x38 cm	1 qt.	1.2 L
11x17 inch	28x43 cm	1 1/4 qt.	1.5 L
8x2 inch round	20x5 cm	1 2/3 qt.	2 L
9x2 inch round	22x5 cm	2 qt.	2.5 L
10x4 1/2 inch tube	25x11 cm	4 1/4 qt.	5 L
8x4x3 inch loaf	20x10x7 cm	1 1/4 qt.	1.5 L
9x5x3 inch loaf	23x12x7 cm	1 2/3 qt.	2 L

INDEX

If you don't see Company's Coming where you shop, ask your retailer to give us a call. Meanwhile, we offer a mail order service for your convenience.

Just indicate the books you would like below. Then complete the reverse page and send your order with payment to us.

Buying a gift? Enclose a personal note or card and we will be pleased to send it with your order.

Deduct $5.00 for every $35.00 ordered.

See reverse.

SAVE $5.00!

Company's Coming COOKBOOKS

Company's Coming Publishing Limited
Box 8037, Station F
Edmonton, Alberta, Canada T6H 4N9
Tel: (403) 450-6223

MAIL ORDER COUPON

QUANTITY • HARD COVER BOOK •

		TOTAL BOOKS	TOTAL PRICE
	Jean Paré's Favorites - Volume One		

TOTAL $17.95 + $1.50 shipping = **$19.45 each** x ____ = $ _____

ENGLISH

QUANTITY • SOFT COVER BOOKS •

150 Delicious Squares		Pasta	
Casseroles		Cakes	
Muffins & More		Barbecues	
Salads		Dinners of the World	
Appetizers		Lunches	
Desserts		Pies	
Soups & Sandwiches		Light Recipes	
Holiday Entertaining		Microwave Cooking	
Cookies		Preserves *(April, 1994)*	
Vegetables			TOTAL BOOKS / TOTAL PRICE
Main Courses			

TOTAL $10.95 + $1.50 shipping = **$12.45 each** x ____ = $ _____

QUANTITY • PINT SIZE BOOKS •

		TOTAL BOOKS	TOTAL PRICE
Finger Food			
Party Planning			
Buffets			

TOTAL $4.99 + $1.00 shipping = **$5.99 each** x ____ = $ _____

FRENCH

QUANTITY • SOFT COVER BOOKS •

150 délicieux carrés		Recettes légères	
Les casseroles		Les salades	
Muffins et plus		La cuisson au micro-ondes	
Les dîners		Les pâtes	
Les barbecues		Les conserves *(avril 1994)*	
Les tartes			TOTAL BOOKS / TOTAL PRICE
Délices des fêtes			

TOTAL $10.95 + $1.50 shipping = **$12.45 each** x ____ = $ _____

Please fill in reverse side of this coupon | **TOTAL PRICE FOR ALL BOOKS** *(See reverse)* * $ _____

Deduct $5.00 for every $35.00 ordered.

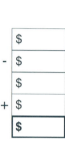

Company's Coming COOKBOOKS

Company's Coming Publishing Limited
Box 8037, Station F
Edmonton, Alberta, Canada T6H 4N9
Tel: (403) 450-6223

MAIL ORDER COUPON

TOTAL PRICE FOR ALL BOOKS (from reverse)	$
Less $5.00 for every $35.00 ordered	- $
SUBTOTAL	$
Canadian residents add G.S.T.	+ $
TOTAL AMOUNT ENCLOSED	$

- **ORDERS OUTSIDE CANADA:** *Must be paid in U.S. funds by cheque or money order drawn on Canadian or U.S. bank.*

- *Prices subject to change without prior notice.*

- *Sorry, no C.O.D.'s*

- **MAKE CHEQUE OR MONEY ORDER PAYABLE TO:** *COMPANY'S COMING PUBLISHING LIMITED*

Gift Giving
We Make It Easy...You Make It Delicious

Let us help you with your gift giving! We will send cookbooks directly to the recipients of your choice if you give us their names and addresses. Be sure to specify the titles of the cookbooks you wish to send to each person.

Send the Company's Coming Cookbooks listed on the reverse side of this coupon to:

Name:

Street:

City: Province/State:

Postal Code/Zip: Tel: (   )   —

Company's Coming Cookbooks make excellent gifts. Birthdays, bridal showers, Mother's Day, Father's Day, graduation or any occasion... collect them all! Remember to enclose your personal note or card and we will be pleased to send it with your order.

If you don't see Company's Coming where you shop, ask your retailer to give us a call. Meanwhile, we offer a mail order service for your convenience.

Just indicate the books you would like below. Then complete the reverse page and send your order with payment to us.

Buying a gift? Enclose a personal note or card and we will be pleased to send it with your order.

Deduct $5.00 for every $35.00 ordered.
See reverse.

SAVE $5.00!

Company's Coming
COOKBOOKS

Company's Coming Publishing Limited
Box 8037, Station F
Edmonton, Alberta, Canada T6H 4N9
Tel: (403) 450-6223

MAIL ORDER COUPON

QUANTITY • HARD COVER BOOK •

	TOTAL BOOKS	TOTAL PRICE
Jean Paré's Favorites - Volume One		
TOTAL $17.95 + $1.50 shipping = **$19.45 each** x	=	$

QUANTITY • SOFT COVER BOOKS •

				TOTAL BOOKS	TOTAL PRICE
	150 Delicious Squares		Pasta		
	Casseroles		Cakes		
	Muffins & More		Barbecues		
	Salads		Dinners of the World		
	Appetizers		Lunches		
	Desserts		Pies		
	Soups & Sandwiches		Light Recipes		
	Holiday Entertaining		Microwave Cooking		
	Cookies		Preserves (April, 1994)		
	Vegetables			TOTAL BOOKS	TOTAL PRICE
	Main Courses				
TOTAL $10.95 + $1.50 shipping = **$12.45 each** x				=	$

QUANTITY • PINT SIZE BOOKS •

			TOTAL BOOKS	TOTAL PRICE
	Finger Food			
	Party Planning		TOTAL BOOKS	TOTAL PRICE
	Buffets			
TOTAL $4.99 + $1.00 shipping = **$5.99 each** x			=	$

QUANTITY • SOFT COVER BOOKS •

				TOTAL BOOKS	TOTAL PRICE
	150 délicieux carrés		Recettes légères		
	Les casseroles		Les salades		
	Muffins et plus		La cuisson au micro-ondes		
	Les dîners		Les pâtes		
	Les barbecues		Les conserves (avril 1994)		
	Les tartes			TOTAL BOOKS	TOTAL PRICE
	Délices des fêtes				
TOTAL $10.95 + $1.50 shipping = **$12.45 each** x				=	$

Please fill in reverse side of this coupon *	TOTAL PRICE FOR ALL BOOKS (See reverse) *	$

SAVE $5.00!

Deduct $5.00 for every $35.00 ordered.

Company's Coming COOKBOOKS

Company's Coming Publishing Limited
Box 8037, Station F
Edmonton, Alberta, Canada T6H 4N9
Tel: (403) 450-6223

MAIL ORDER COUPON

TOTAL PRICE FOR ALL BOOKS (from reverse)	$
Less $5.00 for every $35.00 ordered	− $
SUBTOTAL	$
Canadian residents add G.S.T.	+ $
TOTAL AMOUNT ENCLOSED	$

- **ORDERS OUTSIDE CANADA:** *Must be paid in U.S. funds by cheque or money order drawn on Canadian or U.S. bank.*
- *Prices subject to change without prior notice.*
- *Sorry, no C.O.D.'s*
- **MAKE CHEQUE OR MONEY ORDER PAYABLE TO:** *COMPANY'S COMING PUBLISHING LIMITED*

Gift Giving

We Make It Easy...You Make It Delicious

Let us help you with your gift giving! We will send cookbooks directly to the recipients of your choice if you give us their names and addresses. Be sure to specify the titles of the cookbooks you wish to send to each person.

Send the Company's Coming Cookbooks listed on the reverse side of this coupon to:

Name: _____

Street: _____

City: _____ Province/State: _____

Postal Code/Zip: _____ Tel: (___) ___ — ___

Company's Coming Cookbooks make excellent gifts. Birthdays, bridal showers, Mother's Day, Father's Day, graduation or any occasion... collect them all! Remember to enclose your personal note or card and we will be pleased to send it with your order.